"Mastering Relational Databases: From Fundamentals to Advanced Concepts"

GoodMan, Volume 1

Patrick Mukosha

Published by Patrick Mukosha, 2023.

Title: "Mastering Relational Databases: *From Fundamentals to Advanced Concepts*"

Copyright Notice

International Standard Book Number:

First published: October 2023

Publisher: Patrick Chisenga Mukosha PhD

Trademarks

All terms mentioned in this book that are known to be trademarks or service marks have been appropriately capitalized. The Author and the publisher cannot attest to the accuracy of this information. Use of a term in this book should not be regarded as affecting the validity of any trademark or service mark.

Warning and Disclaimer

Every effort has been made to make this book as complete and as accurate as possible, but no warranty or fitness is implied. The information provided in this book is on as is basis. The Author and the Publisher shall have neither liability nor responsibility to any person or entity with respect to any loss or damage arising from the use the information contained in this book.

Author: Patrick Chisenga Mukosha PhD

Acknowledgements

The author is indebted to a large number of researchers, and consultants in the field of Relational Databases whose works were referred to in writing this book – and appears below and in the bibliography.

The author also would like to acknowledge the encouragement of my wife; Gracious Lumba Maboshe-Mukosha, my colleagues Bernard Chisanga (MHSRIP) and Dr Thomas Mabwe (MHSRIP), and my children, whose comments and constructive criticism kept the author alive. The author also benefitted from the comments of my colleague: Satish Raju and James Milner. He generously shared his insights and experiences in an evolving field where tacit knowledge is indispensable.

The author wishes to thank his late Father; Isaac Mulando Mukosha (MHSRIP) and mother; Rebecca Mukosha (MHSRIP), for their endless love.

Special thanks go to Lionel Hugh Weston; my former Secondary School Teacher and Guardian, without whom I would never have had a strong education foundation in life. His contribution in my education career is immeasurable. I shall forever remain indebted to him and the entire Weston's family.

Abstract

"Mastering Relational Databases: *From Fundamentals to Advanced Concepts*" is an indispensable guide for anyone seeking to become an expert in the world of relational databases. This comprehensive book takes readers on a journey from the very basics of relational databases to advanced topics, equipping them with the knowledge and skills needed to effectively design, manage, and optimize database systems.

Key Features:

1. **Fundamental Concepts:** The book begins with a solid foundation, covering the fundamental concepts of relational databases. Readers will gain a clear understanding of what databases are, how they work, and why they are crucial in the world of data management.
2. **Data Modelling:** It delves deep into data modelling techniques, teaching readers how to design efficient and normalized database schemas. Concepts like entities, attributes, relationships, and normalization are explained in a practical and accessible manner.
3. **SQL Mastery:** The book provides a comprehensive guide to Structured Query Language (SQL), covering everything from basic queries to advanced topics like stored procedures, triggers, and optimization techniques. Readers will learn to harness the full power of SQL to manipulate and retrieve data effectively.
4. **Indexing and Performance Optimisation:** Performance is a critical aspect of database management. The book explores advanced techniques for indexing, query optimization, and database tuning, ensuring that readers can maximize the efficiency of their database systems.
5. **Concurrency Control and Transactions:** Understanding how databases handle multiple users and ensure data consistency is essential. This book explains concurrency control mechanisms and the principles of transaction management in depth.
6. **Security and Data Integrity:** Security is paramount in modern databases. The book covers authentication, authorization, encryption, and data integrity mechanisms, enabling readers to protect their data from

unauthorized access and breaches.

7. **Advanced Topics:** For those looking to push the boundaries, the book explores advanced topics such as distributed databases, replication, and high availability solutions, ensuring readers are well-prepared to tackle complex real-world scenarios.
8. **Practical Example:** Throughout the book, practical examples and real-world case studies illustrate key concepts, making it easy for readers to apply what they've learned in their own database projects.
9. **Best Practices:** The book emphasizes best practices in database design, administration, and maintenance, instilling a professional approach to managing data.

"Mastering Relational Databases: *From Fundamentals to Advanced Concepts*" is not just a book; it's a comprehensive resource that empowers readers to become proficient in all aspects of relational databases. Whether you are a beginner looking to grasp the basics or an experienced database professional seeking to refine your skills, this book will be your go-to reference on the journey to mastering relational databases.

1. Introduction to Relational Databases

The relational model (RM) of databases, first introduced by English computer scientist Edgar F. Codd in 1970, is a method for managing data that adheres to a structure and language consistent with first-order predicate logic. All data is represented as tuples that are organized into relations. A relational database is one that is set up using the relational model.

A table is created by grouping data into rows and columns in a relational database. Usually, data is organized into different tables that can be linked together using a primary key or a foreign key. These distinct identifiers show the many connections that exist across tables; these connections are typically shown through various kinds of data models. By combining various data points and summarizing business performance, analysts utilize SQL queries to help firms obtain new perspectives, streamline processes, and spot untapped opportunities.

Consider a scenario in which your business keeps a database table of customer data that includes account-level corporate information. Another table that lists every single transaction that corresponds to that account may also exist. When combined, these tables can reveal details about the various markets for a certain software product.

Customer ID, Company Name, Company Address, Industry, etc., might be the columns (or fields) for the customer table. Conversely, the columns for a transaction table could be Transaction Date, Customer ID, Transaction Amount, Payment Method, etc. The shared Customer ID field allows the tables to be connected. As a result, you may query the table to get useful information, including sales figures by industry or firm, which can guide message to potential customers.

Transactional databases, which execute orders or transactions collectively, are frequently linked to relational databases. A bank transfer is a frequent example that is used to demonstrate this. A specific amount is taken out of one account and deposited into another.

Money is withdrawn and placed in whole, and no partial withdrawals or deposits are allowed during this transaction. Transactions have particular characteristics.

The following are examples of the acronym "ACID" properties:

- *Atomicity:* The treatment of all data changes as a single operation. That is, either every change is made or none of them are.
- *Consistency:* Data integrity is strengthened by consistency, which ensures that data is in the same condition from start to finish.
- *Isolation:* Because other transactions cannot see a transaction's intermediate state, concurrent transactions appear to be serialized.
- *Durability:* Changes to data that have been successfully completed after a transaction persist and cannot be undone, even in the event of a system failure.

These characteristics make transaction processing dependable.

a. The Significance of Relational Databases

Relational databases play a crucial role in many facets of business, technology, and data administration. They are a fundamental part of contemporary information systems. The fundamental advantage of a relational database is its capacity to link data from many tables to provide insightful data. This strategy aids businesses of all sizes and sectors in identifying connections between multiple data sets from various departments to produce insightful information.

Therefore, the capacity to produce meaningful information by combining the tables is the main advantage of the relational database strategy. Understanding the relationships between the data or how the tables are connected is made possible by joining the tables. SQL has the capacity to add, combine, group, and count queries. Basic math, subtotal functions, and logical transformations can all be carried out with SQL. Results can be sorted by date, name, or any other column for analysts. The relational approach is currently the most widely used query tool in business thanks to these capabilities.

Key elements of their relevance are as follows:

1. **Data Organization and Structure:** Relational databases offer a structured and organized method of managing and storing the data. Because data is saved in tables with predetermined schemas, consistency and integrity in data storage are maintained.
2. **Data Integrity**: By enforcing data integrity through restrictions and regulations, they make sure that the data entered into the database is correct, consistent, and meets predetermined criteria. By doing this, errors and data corruption are avoided.
3. **Querying and Retrieval**: Relational databases have strong

querying capabilities, enabling users to quickly access, filter, and analyse data. Relational databases can be accessed using the standard language known as SQL (Structured Query Language).

4. **Scalability:** In order to accommodate growing data loads and user concurrency, relational databases can scale both vertically (by adding server resources) and horizontally (by splitting data across several servers).
5. **ACID Properties:** The ACID (Atomicity, Consistency, Isolation, Durability) properties they offer transactional support make sure that database operations are dependable and maintain data consistency.
6. **Data Relationships:** Relational databases are excellent at maintaining intricate relationships between data elements. They provide effective data retrieval and maintenance by allowing the formation of foreign keys and defining relationships between tables.
7. **Security:** Relational database management systems (RDBMS) are often developed with strong security measures, such as user authentication, authorization, and encryption, to secure sensitive data.
8. **Data Analysis and Reporting:** Relational databases are the cornerstone of data warehousing and business intelligence solutions, which in turn serve as the basis for data analysis and reporting. Using SQL queries, analysts can run complex data analyses and produce reports.
9. **Data Integration**: By offering a single platform for data storage and retrieval, they make it easier to integrate data from many sources. For applications that need to access several data sets, this is essential.
10. **Historical Data:** Relational databases are ideal for storing historical data because they enable businesses to monitor

changes in their data over time.

11. **Compliance and Auditing**: Relational databases assist firms in meeting compliance requirements in regulated sectors like healthcare and finance by offering auditing.
12. **Data Backup and Recovery**: RDBMSs have facilities for automated data backup and recovery, which lowers the chance of data loss due to hardware failures or user error.
13. **Transaction Processing**: Relational databases are frequently used in high-frequency transaction processing applications, including e-commerce, banking, and inventory management.
14. **Data Consistency in Applications:** They include techniques like foreign keys and referential integrity, which help maintain data quality and reliability, to assure data consistency in applications.
15. **Legacy Systems:** Relational databases are essential for maintaining and updating legacy systems because so many programs and systems now in use are built on them.

Thus, relational databases are essential for handling structured data, guaranteeing data integrity, facilitating data analysis, and enabling the effective operation of a variety of applications and businesses. It is impossible to exaggerate their importance in the fields of information technology and data management.

b. Historical Development of Relational Databases

Relational databases have had a remarkable historical development over many years. Here is a brief summary of the significant turning points and advancements in relational database history:

1. **Pre-Relational Database Era 1940s–1960s:** Early data management initiatives relied on rigid flat files and hierarchical databases that couldn't adequately reflect complex relationships.
2. **Codd's Proposition (1969):** With the release of Dr. Edgar F. Codd's seminal work, "A Relational Model of Data for Large Shared Data Banks," which first popularized the idea of a relational database model, the contemporary relational database era officially began. The Codd's model introduced the idea of using a query language to interact with the data and suggested presenting data as tables (relations) with rows and columns.
3. **SQL and System R from the 1970s:** One of the first applications of the relational model was the IBM System R project, which was started in the 1970s. For communicating with relational databases, Structured Query Language (SQL) was created as a standard language.
4. **Relational Database Commercialization (1970s–1980s):** Relational database management systems (RDBMS) were first offered commercially by organizations like IBM, Oracle, and Ingres. In 1979, Oracle, the first commercial RDBMS from Oracle Corporation, was made available.
5. **SQL Standards (1980s–1990s)**: There is now more compatibility across various relational database systems because to the development of SQL standards by ANSI and

ISO. The standards' SQL-86, SQL-89, and SQL-92 versions were significant turning points.

6. **Client-Server Architecture (1980s):** Relational databases were used as the backends for many different applications, and the client-server architecture gained popularity.
7. **Object-Relational Databases (1990s):** With the development of object-relational databases (ORDBMS), relational database functionality was combined with support for sophisticated data types and object-oriented programming ideas.
8. **Relational Open Source Databases (since the 2000s):** Due to their affordability and comprehensive feature sets, open-source RDBMSs like MySQL and PostgreSQL have grown in popularity. Particularly recognized for its versatility and support for complex data types is PostgreSQL.
9. **Big Data and NoSQL (from the 2000s):** Big data's emergence sparked the creation of NoSQL databases, which are built to manage enormous amounts of unstructured or semi-structured data. For particular use scenarios, these databases provide an alternative to conventional relational databases.
10. **Cloud-Based Databases (since the 2010s):** Managed relational database services are available through cloud computing platforms like Amazon Web Services (AWS) and Microsoft Azure, making scaling and administration of databases easier.
11. **(Since the 2010s) NewSQL:** The scalability of NoSQL databases and the ACID transactional capabilities of conventional RDBMSs are combined in NewSQL databases.
12. **Integration of AI and Machine Learning (2010s–Present):** For data analysis and predictive modelling, modern RDBMSs increasingly incorporate machine learning and artificial

intelligence capabilities.

13. **Distributed Databases and Blockchain Technology (2010s–Present):** Emerging technologies like blockchain make use of relational distributed databases to offer safe, decentralized data storage.

The historical history of relational databases demonstrates the development of data management as well as the relational model's continuing applicability and adaptability in a constantly evolving technical environment. Along with other data storage and processing technologies, relational databases continue to be an essential part of data management in many different businesses today.

Chapter 1: Fundamentals of Relational Databases

1.1 What Is a Relational Database?

A *Relational Database* is a database that uses the relational model of data, which was first put forth by E. F. Codd in 1970. A *Relational Database Management System* (RDBMS) is a program used to keep relational databases up to date. Many relational database systems allow users to query and update the database using SQL (Structured Query Language).

The relational model's goal is to offer a declarative method for specifying data and queries. Users directly state what information the database contains and what information they want from it, and they delegate the description of data structures for storing the data and retrieval procedures for responding to queries to the database management system software.

The SQL data definition and query language, which is used by the majority of relational databases, implements what might be thought of as an engineering approximation to the relational model. In a SQL database structure, a table represents a predicate variable, a table's data represents a relation, and key constraints, other restrictions, and SQL queries represent predicates. However, SQL databases depart greatly from the relational paradigm, and Codd vehemently fought against departures that subvert the fundamental ideas.

An example of a relational database is a database management system (DBMS) that arranges and stores data in an organized way in accordance with the relational data model's guiding principles. Data is kept in tables with rows and columns in a relational database, and these tables can be coupled to one another through predefined relationships.

The essential elements and traits of a relational database are as follows:

1.1.1 **Tables:** A relational database's basic building block is a table. They are made up of columns and rows. Every table represents a certain entity or kind of information, such as clients, orders, goods, personnel, etc. In a table, the rows stand in for specific records or instances of data, while the columns represent the qualities or characteristics of those entries.

1.1.2 **Records and Rows**: Records, sometimes referred to as tuples or rows, house the actual data entries. A table's rows each represent a single data entity or record. For instance, every row in a "Customers" table can correspond to a different client.

1.1.3 **Columns and Attributes:** A table's columns and attributes specify the kinds of data that can be stored inside. A specific attribute or property of the data items is represented by one or more columns. For instance, you might have columns for "CustomerID," "FirstName," "LastName," "Email," and so on in a "Customers" database.

1.1.4 **Primary Key:** A primary key is a number that uniquely identifies every record in a table. It guarantees that every row has a distinct identity. Customer IDs, product IDs, or social security numbers are examples of frequently used primary keys.

1.1.5 **Foreign Key**: A foreign key is a column that connects the primary key of one table to another table's primary key. In order to link related data from several tables together, this connection is employed. An "Orders" table, for instance, may have a foreign key connecting it to the "Customers" table.

1.1.6 **Table Relationships:** The connections between main and foreign keys define the connections between tables. One-to-one, one-to-many, and many-to-many connections are frequent types of relationships.

1.1.7 **SQL (Structured Query Language):** The standard language for interacting with relational databases is SQL (Structured Query Language). Users can query, insert, update, and delete data, among other activities, with this tool.

1.1.8 **Data Integrity Constraints:** Relational databases use constraints to protect data integrity, such as check constraints, referential integrity constraints, and uniqueness requirements. These limitations aid in maintaining the consistency and accuracy of the data in the database.

1.1.9 **ACID Properties:** Relational databases are renowned for supporting the ACID qualities (Atomicity, Consistency, Isolation, Durability), which ensure that database transactions are trustworthy and uphold data integrity.

1.1.10 **Normalization:** To lessen redundancy and increase data integrity, normalization is the act of structuring data in a database. To avoid duplicate data, it entails splitting up big tables into smaller, relevant ones.

1.1.11 **Indexes:** Data structures called indexes are used to speed up data retrieval procedures. They provide quicker data retrieval and searches based on particular columns.

Because they can store structured data, create relationships between data elements, and offer robust querying capabilities, relational databases are widely utilized in many applications and sectors. They are crucial tools for effectively managing and organizing data.

1.2 Components of a Relational Database System

Multiple layers and important parts make up a relational database system, which is used to organize and alter data.

These elements consist of:

1.2.1 **Database:** The top-level container for all the information and metadata pertaining to a specific application or domain is the database. It functions as a logical division for managing and organizing data. Schemas are a subset of databases that can be further broken into smaller parts.

1.2.2 **Schema:** Tables, views, procedures, and other database objects are logically grouped together in a database container called a schema. It aids in classifying and separating various database components. For instance, you might have distinct schemas for books, users, and transactions in a database for a library system.

1.2.3 **Tables:** A relational database's basic building elements are tables. They use rows and columns to hold data. Each table depicts a certain entity or type of data, such as clients, goods, or orders. The properties and structure of the data in tables are specified.

1.2.4 **Columns:** The types of data that can be recorded in a table are determined by columns, which are often referred to as fields or attributes. Each column in the table represents a different property of the data items there. Columns in a "Customers" table might include "CustomerID," "FirstName," "LastName," and "Email." as an illustration.

1.2.5 **Rows:** Individual data instances or records within a table are represented by rows, which are also known as records or tuples. Each row has data values that correspond to the table's declared columns. One client may be represented by a single row in a "*Customers*" table with values for each column.

1.2.6 **Primary Keys:** Columns or groups of columns known as *Primary Keys* are used to uniquely identify each row in a table. They make sure that the table contains an individual identifier for each record. The preservation of data integrity and the creation of connections between tables depend on primary keys.

1.2.7 **Foreign Keys:** Columns in one table that refer to the primary key of another table are known as "*Foreign Keys.*" They create connections between tables, allowing for data integrity and the retrieval of related data. Referential integrity is enforced through foreign keys.

1.2.8 **Indexes:** These are data structures that speed up processes like searching and sorting that involve retrieving data. They give easy access to particular rows based on the contents of one or more columns.

1.2.9 **SQL (Structured Query Language):** The standard language for interacting with relational databases is SQL (Structured Query Language). It offers instructions for creating and altering database objects as well as for querying, inserting, updating, and removing data.

1.2.10 **Database Management System (DBMS):** The DBMS is a piece of software that administers and regulates database access. For building, managing, and communicating with the database, it offers tools and services. MySQL, PostgreSQL, Microsoft SQL Server, Oracle Database, and SQLite are examples of popular relational DBMSs.

1.2.11 **Data Integrity Constraints:** Rules governing data accuracy and consistency within the database are known as data integrity constraints. Uniqueness requirements (ensuring that values are unique), referential integrity constraints (enforcing relationships between tables), and check constraints (definition of specific data validation methods) are examples of common constraints.

1.2.12 **Transaction Management:** Relational database systems include support for transaction management, which makes sure that a series of database actions is carried out atomically (all at once). To preserve data integrity, transactions abide by the ACID properties (Atomicity, Consistency, Isolation, and Durability).

1.2.13 **Security and Authentication:** Access to databases is restricted using security features built into database systems. To protect sensitive data, this requires user authentication, authorization, and access control.

1.2.14 **Database Management System (DBMS)**

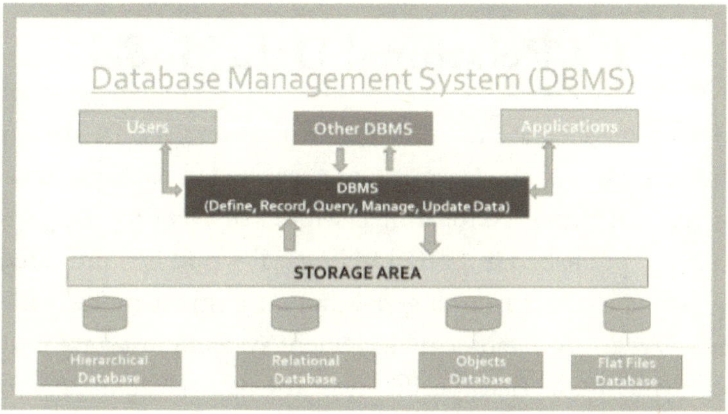

Figure 1: Database Management System (DBMS), Copyright: Patrick Mukosha (2023), "Mastering Relational Databases: From Fundamentals to Advanced Concepts"

These elements come together to form a structured and effective environment for relational database storage, management, and retrieval. An important factor in a relational database system's overall performance and dependability is how these components are designed and managed.

1.3 Relational Data Model

A key idea in database administration is the relational data model, which specifies how data is set up and organised in relational databases. In his seminal paper "A Relational Model of Data for Large Shared Data Banks" published in 1970, Dr. Edgar F. Codd first proposed it.

A database's data is arranged using an abstract model called the *relational model.* A database management system must have some sort of underlying model that specifies how the data within it are arranged in order to regulate access to a database, write data, conduct queries, or carry out any other database administration-related actions.

Relational databases are typically used to refer to *databases that use the relational paradigm.* The development of non-relational, or NoSQL, data models has only lately slowed down the widespread adoption of the relational model, which for a long time dominated the field of data organization.

Relationships are the most fundamental components of the relational model, and users and contemporary RDBMSs refer to relations as tables. A relation is a collection of tuples, or table rows, each of which shares a set of attributes, or table columns. The simplest unit of organization in a relational database is a column, which stands in for the numerous characteristics that characterize the records in the table. They are called characteristics in a more formal manner. Consider each tuple as a distinct instance of any individuals, things, occasions, or associations the database contains.

The following fundamental ideas and principles define the relational data model:

1.3.1 **Tables (Relations):** Data is structured into tables, which are often referred to as relations, in the relational data paradigm. Each table represents a specific entity or concept, such as customers, orders, products, or employees. Tables consist of rows and columns.

1.3.2 **Rows (Tuples):** In a table, rows, also referred to as tuples, stand in for individual data records. According to the attributes (columns) specified for that table, each row comprises a set of values. For instance, every row in a "Customers" table can correspond to a different client.

1.3.3 **Columns (Attributes):** The sorts of data that can be recorded in a table are determined by its columns, commonly referred to as attributes or fields. In the table, each column represents a certain property or attribute of the data items. A "Customers" table, for instance, might have the columns "CustomerID," "FirstName," "LastName," and "Email."

1.3.4 **Primary Key:** In a table, the one or more columns known as the primary key serve to uniquely identify each row. It makes sure that every record has a distinctive identifier, which is essential for maintaining data integrity and creating connections between databases.

1.3.5 **Foreign Key:** A foreign key is a column that points to the main key of another table in one table. It creates connections between tables, enabling data linking and guaranteeing referential integrity. Foreign keys aid in keeping the database consistent.

1.3.6 **Data Integrity:** Through constraints and rules, the relational data model imposes data integrity. These restrictions include check constraints (which provide data validation standards), primary key constraints (which enforce uniqueness), foreign key constraints (which maintain relationships), and more.

1.3.7 **Relationships:** The foundation of the relational data model are relationships between tables. They show how primary and foreign keys link to or connect distinct tables to one another. The three most common sorts of relationships are one-to-one, one-to-many, and many-to-many.

1.3.8 **Normalization:** The process of structuring data in a way that lessens data redundancy and enhances data integrity is known as normalization. It is a crucial component of the relational paradigm and includes splitting huge tables into smaller, related tables.

1.3.9 **Structured Query Language (SQL):** Relational databases can be accessed using the structured query language (SQL), which is a standardized language. It offers instructions for creating and altering database objects as well as for querying, inserting, updating, and removing data.

1.3.10 **ACID Properties:** Relational databases follow the ACID principles of atomicity, consistency, isolation, and durability (Atomicity, Consistency, Isolation, Durability) to make sure that database transactions are trustworthy, maintain data consistency, and are resilient to errors.

1.3.11 **Flexibility:** The relational model is adaptable and can deal with a variety of data kinds and intricate data structures. It has been widely adopted across many industries and is highly suited for structured data.

The majority of commercial database management systems (DBMS) are built on the relational data model, which has been an essential component of information systems and data management for decades. It is a crucial idea in the area of database technology because it offers a systematic and effective approach to organize, store, and retrieve data.

1.4 Structured Query Language (SQL)

Structured Query Language (SQL), developed by Don Chamberlin and Ray Boyce at IBM, is the industry-standard programming language for communicating with relational database management systems. It enables database administrators to quickly add, amend, or delete rows of data. Due to a trademark issue, it was previously named as SEQUEL but was later abbreviated to SQL. Users can also obtain data from databases using SQL queries by writing very little code. It is simple to understand why relational databases are occasionally referred to as "SQL databases" given this link.

Relational databases are managed and worked on using the standardized programming language; Structured Query Language (SQL). For executing different database activities, such as querying data, inserting, updating, and removing data, establishing and altering database structures, and controlling user access and permissions, SQL offers a set of commands and syntax.

The relational database is created, maintained, and retrieved using the structured query language, which is a common database language. We shall go into detail regarding SQL in this chapter. Here are some intriguing SQL-related statistics. Pay attention to that. SQL doesn't care about case. However, it is advised to capitalize keywords (such as '**SELECT**', '**UPDATE**', and '**CREATE**') and use tiny letters for user-defined terms (such as table and column names).

Using the double hyphen character "—" at the start of any line, we can enter comments in SQL. The programming language used by relational databases like MySQL, Oracle, Sybase, SQL Server, Postgre, etc. is called SQL. SQL is not used by other non-relational databases, commonly known as NoSQL databases, such as MongoDB, DynamoDB, etc.

Although SQL has an ISO standard, the majority of implementations have a little bit of a different syntax. Consequently, we can run into queries that work in SQL Server but not in MySQL.

These are some essential features of SQL:

1. **Querying Data:** The '**SELECT**' statement in SQL enables users to get data from a database. Using operations like '**WHERE**', '**ORDER BY**', and '**GROUP BY**', users can specify which columns to obtain, filter data based on criteria, sort results, and group data.

Example:

```
SELECT FirstName, LastName FROM Customers WHERE Country =
'USA' ORDER BY LastName;
```

1. **Insert Data:** The '**INSERT**' statement is used to add new rows of data to a table.

Example:

```
INSERT INTO Products (ProductID, ProductName, Price) VALUE (161,
'Widget', 25.50);
```

1. **Update Data:** The '**UPDATE**' statement is used in SQL to modify existing data in a table.

Example:

```
UPDATE Employees SET Salary = 14500 WHERE EmployeeID = 115;
```

1. **Deleting Data:** The **'DELETE'** statement is used in SQL to remove rows from existing data in a table, based on specified conditions.

Example:

```
DELETE FROM Orders WHERE OrderID = 543;
```

1. **Creating and Modifying Tables:** SQL provides commands to create new database tables (**'CREATE TABLE'**) and modify existing table structures (**'ALTER TABLE'**). Users can define columns, data types, constraints, and relationships between tables.

Example: (Table Creation):

```
CREATE TABLE Customers (
    CustomerID INT PRIMARY KEY,
    FirstName VARCHAR (50),
    LastName VARCHAR (50),
    Email VARCHAR (50),
);
```

1. **Data Integrity Constraints:** SQL allows the definition of constraints to enforce data integrity rules, such as uniqueness

(**'UNIQUE'**), primary keys (**'PRIMARY KEY'**) and foreign keys (**'FOREIGN KEY'**).

Example: (Constraint Definition):

```
CREATE TABLE Orders (
        OrderID INT PRIMARY KEY,
        CustomerID INT,
        OrderDate VINT,
        Email VARCHAR (50),
        FOREIGN KEY (CustomerID) RFERENCES Customers
        (CustomerID)
);
```

1. **Aggregation and Grouping:** SQL supports aggregation functions like **'SUM'**, **'AVG'**, **'COUNT'**, and **'MAX'** to perform calculations on data. These functions are often used with the **'GROUP BY'** clause to summarise data.

Example: (Aggregation):

```
SELECT Category, AVG (Price) AS AvgPrice FROM Products GROUP BY
Category;
```

1. **Joins:** SQL enables the combination of data from multiple tables using **'JOIN'** operations. Common types of joins include **'INNER JOIN'**, **'LEFT JOIN'**, and **'RIGHT JOIN'**.

Example: (INNER JOIN):

```
SELECT Orders.OrderID, Customers.FirstName
FROM Orders
INNER JOIN Customers ON Orders.CustomerID; =
Customers.CustomerID;
```

1. **Transaction Control:** SQL provides commands for

managing transactions, including **'BEGIN TRANSACTION'**, **'COMMIT'**, and **'ROLLBACK'**, which are used to ensure data consistency and reliability in multi-step operations.

Many different database management systems, including MySQL, PostgreSQL, Microsoft SQL Server, Oracle Database, and SQLite, among others, provide SQL, a potent tool for working with relational databases. It is a crucial language for anyone interested in database building, administration, or data analysis due to its uniform syntax and wide range of capabilities.

Chapter 2: Fundamentals of Relational Databases

2.1 Entity-Relationship Diagrams (ERDs)

A database's structure and relationships of entities are shown visually in *Entity-Relationship Diagrams* (ERDs). They are frequently used in database modelling and design to show how various entities link to one another. To represent entities, characteristics, relationships, and constraints, ERDs employ a variety of symbols and notations.

Thus, an ERD is a sort of diagram that *demonstrates the relationships* between various entities (such as employees, users, clients, or other objects) in an application or database. They are made when a new system is being designed so that the database's structure can be understood by the development team. They can also be built on an existing system to assist the team in figuring out how it operates and identifying and fixing any problems. Entity Relationship Diagrams represent the system and database using a particular set of symbols, such as shapes and arrows.

The following are the main elements and ideas of ERDs:

2.1.1 Entities: In a database, real-world objects, ideas, or other items are represented by entities. In an ERD, each entity is often represented by a rectangle. The terms "customer," "product," "order," "employee," etc. are examples of entities. A strong entity has a unique identifier (a *Primary Key*) and does not require the existence of any other things. An employee, for instance, might be a strong entity because it can have a primary key and doesn't require the existence of any other things. A weak entity is one whose existence is dependent on a strong entity. It has a *Foreign Key* to another entity, according to this. For instance, an employee's department may be a weak entity because an employee is required for department to exist.

2.1.2 Attributes: The qualities or properties of an entity are its attributes. They describe the information connected to an entity. Typically, attributes are shown as connected ovals to the appropriate entities. For instance, the characteristics of an entity called "Customer" might include "CustomerID," "FirstName," "LastName," and "Email."

2.1.3 Relationships: Relationships show connections between different kinds of things. They explain the relationships between the various entities. Relationships are represented as lines joining objects, with labels describing their nature. Relationships that are frequently found are "one-to-one," "one-to-many," and "many-to-many."

2.1.4 One-to-One (1:1): One instance of an entity in Entity A is linked to an instance of an entity in Entity B, and vice versa. One "Person" might, for instance, have one "Passport," and one "Passport" might be that "Person."

2.1.5 One-to-Many (1:N): One instance of an entity in Entity A is linked to numerous instances of that entity in Entity B. As an illustration, a "Department" could have several "Employees," but each "Employee" is a part of a single "Department."

2.1.6 Many-to-Many (N:M): numerous entity instances in Entity A are linked to numerous entity instances in Entity B in a many-to-many (N:M) relationship. An ERD frequently use a junction table or associative entity to depict many-to-many relationships. For instance, "Students" may enrol in multiple "Courses," and there may be several "Students" in each "Course."

2.1.7 Primary Key: A primary key is an attribute (or a combination of characteristics) within an entity that uniquely identifies each entity instance. It is necessary for upholding data integrity and creating connections between entities.

2.1.8 Cardinality: When two entities are associated to one another in a specific connection, the number of instances of one entity that may be related to the number of occurrences of the other entity is known as the "cardinality." Numeral values or notations like "1" (one) or "M" (many) are frequently used to express the concept of cardinality.

2.1.9 Weak Entities: Entities that lack a primary key property on their own are referred to as weak entities. They depend on another organization, referred to as the owning or parent organization, to supply a portion of their primary key.

2.1.10 Associative Entities: Junction tables or linking tables are another name for associative entities, which are used to express many-to-many relationships. They include information about both the relationship and the connected entities.

2.1.11 Derived Attributes: These are attributes whose values can be estimated or extrapolated from those of other attributes in the database. They can be calculated as needed but are normally not saved in the database.

2.1.12 Supertype and Subtype Entities: Supertype and subtype entities are used to model the relationships between entities when they have common attributes as well as unique attributes. The common properties are represented by the supertype entity, while the unique attributes are represented by the subtype entities.

To see a database system's structure, comprehend its relationships, and make sure that the database architecture appropriately reflects the real-world domain it represents, database designers and developers can benefit from using ERDs. They help to create an effective and well-organized database by giving a high-level perspective of the database schema.

2.2 Normalization

The process of normalization in database architecture is arranging data in a way that minimizes data redundancy and guarantees data integrity. Normalization's main objective is to arrange a relational database to get rid of data abnormalities such update anomalies, insertion anomalies, and deletion anomalies while also cutting down on data duplication. Typically, normalization is accomplished in stages, with each stage being represented by a different normal form (e.g., First Normal Form, Second Normal Form, etc.).

The main ideas and phases of normalization are as follows:

2.2.1 1NF, or First Normal Form: In 1NF, every table needs a primary key that identifies every row (record) in a particular way. A table must have atomic (indivisible) values in every column. This means that just one item of information should be stored in each column. Lists, arrays, and other intricate structures should not be placed in columns.

2.2.2 2NF, or Second Normal Form: A table must first meet the standards of 1NF in order to reach 2NF. All non-key attributes (columns), in addition to 1NF, must be completely functionally reliant on the entire main key. By doing this, partial dependencies—where some attributes rely on just a portion of the primary key—are eliminated. To eliminate partial dependencies, tables are typically split into several related tables to achieve 2NF.

2.2.3 3NF, Or Third Normal Form: A table must first meet the conditions of 2NF in order to reach 3NF. Transitive dependencies between non-key characteristics shouldn't exist in 3NF. As a result, attribute A should not depend on attribute C if attribute A depends on attribute B and attribute B depends on attribute C. In order to achieve 3NF, additional tables are frequently created and used to store data with transitive dependencies.

2.2.4 BCNF, or Boyce-Codd Normal Form: A tighter method of normalization called BCNF is used when a table may have many candidate keys, or groups of columns that can each uniquely identify a set of rows. Every non-trivial functional dependency in BCNF requires a superkey as the left-hand side (determinant). A superkey is a group of characteristics that can be used to identify a row exclusively. It may be necessary to further decompose tables in order to achieve BCNF.

2.2.5 4NF or Fourth Normal Form: This is a Multi-valued dependencies, in which the value of one attribute depends on numerous values of a different attribute, are dealt with using 4NF. A table must first meet the standards of 3NF in order to reach 4NF. By constructing distinct tables to express relationships between attributes, multi-valued dependencies are removed.

2.2.6 5NF or Fifth Normal Form: A table that displays join dependencies that span many tables is addressed by 5NF. In order to remove join dependencies and achieve 5NF, tables are frequently divided into smaller tables. It's crucial to remember that not all databases require the same level of normalization. The trade-offs between data consistency and query efficiency and the unique requirements of the application determine the extent of normalization. Database designers must avoid over-normalization because it can result in complex queries and poor performance.

The choice of the normal form to attain during the iterative process of normalization depends on the application's particular data and business needs.

2.3 Data Integrity Constraints

To guarantee the quality, consistency, and dependability of the data in a database, data integrity constraints are enforced. These limitations aid in preserving the accuracy and reliability of the data kept in a relational database. The database management system (DBMS) enforces them to stop incorrect or inconsistent data from being changed or inserted.

Here are some typical restrictions on data integrity:

2.3.1 Principal Key Constraint: Each record in a table has a primary key that serves as a unique identifier. It guarantees that every table row has a distinct identity. Duplicate values in the primary key column(s) are prevented by the primary key constraint. For example, a “CustomerID” in the "Customers" table.

2.3.2 Unique Constraint: A unique constraint guarantees that the values in a certain column (or group of columns) are exclusive across all table rows. It stops duplicate values from being added to the restricted column(s). For illustration, make sure each email address in a "Users" table is distinct.

2.3.3 Foreign Key Constraint: By connecting a column in one table to the primary key in another, a foreign key constraint creates a relationship between the two tables. By requiring that the values in the foreign key column match those in the main key column being referenced, it protects referential integrity. For instance, linking “Order.CustomerID” to “Customer.CustomerID” to guarantee that orders are connected to legitimate consumers.

2.3.4 Check Constraint: A check constraint specifies the requirements that data must satisfy in order to be considered valid. It stops the addition or change of data that doesn't meet the required criteria. For illustration, mandate that the "Birthdate" column only contains dates from the recent past.

2.3.5 Default Constraint: If no value is entered during data entry, a default constraint defines a default value for the column. It makes sure that every row, even if not specifically stated, has a value for the column. Setting "Active" as the default value for the "Status" column in a user profile table is an illustration.

2.3.6 Not Null Constraint: A column cannot have null (missing) values according to a not null constraint. It guarantees that there must be a value in the restricted column for each row. Example: Ensuring that a product identifier always appears in the "ProductID" column of an "Orders" table.

2.3.7 Cascade and Set Null Actions: These restrictions outline the steps to be followed (foreign key actions) when data in a referenced table is modified or deleted. While set null actions set associated foreign key values to null, cascade actions automatically disseminate changes to linked rows. Cascading, for instance, may set the customer ID in connected orders to null or erase associated orders when a client is deleted.

2.3.8 Domain Constraints: The permitted values for a column are determined by domain constraints depending on the required data type or format. It is possible to utilize them to limit values to a particular range or pattern.

Example: Declaring that the postal codes in a "ZipCode" column must be accurate.

Constraints on data integrity are essential for preserving the reliability and consistency of data in a database. They aid in preventing data anomalies that could cause data corruption and mistakes in applications that rely on the database, such as duplicate records, incorrect relationships, and inaccurate values

2.4 Indexing and Optimization

Relational database administration requires indexing and optimization because they enhance query performance and overall database effectiveness. They entail the development of data structures and the application of a number of strategies to quicken data retrieval processes. An overview of relational databases' indexing and optimization is provided below:

2.4.1 Indexing:

2.4.1.1 What is an Index?

A database structure known as an index offers a quick and effective way to look up rows in a table using the values of one or more columns. Consider an index to be similar to a book's index, which enables you to discover certain information quickly without having to read the entire book.

2.4.1.2 Types of Indexes:

- **Single-Column Index:** A single column index. It expedites data filtering and sorting queries that use that column.
- **Composite Index:** A multiple-column index. It helps queries that make use of certain columns in conjunction.
- **Unique Index**: A unique index ensures that each column in an index is unique, preventing duplicate values.
- **Clustered Index:** A table's physical order of data rows is determined by a clustered index. There can only be one clustered index per table.
- **Non-Clustered Index**: A distinct data structure that identifies the precise locations of table entries.
- **Full-material Index:** Used to quickly search material within

lengthy text columns.

2.4.1.3 Creating Indexes: SQL statements like generate INDEX are used to CREATE indexes. Since indexes require storage space and take up space, it is crucial to carefully choose which columns to index.

2.4.1.4 When to Create Indexes: The most efficient usage of indexes in SQL queries is for columns that are frequently utilized in the WHERE, JOIN, and ORDER BY clauses. It's important to achieve a balance because excessive indexing can result in higher storage needs and maintenance costs.

2.4.2 Optimization:

2.4.2.1 Optimization of Query: The process of speeding up a SQL query's execution plan is known as query optimization. Based on the query analysis and statistics and available indexes and execution plans, the database optimizer selects the most effective execution strategy.

2.4.2.2 Statistics: The DBMS keeps statistics on the distribution of data across tables, which the optimizer uses to decide how best to execute queries. For accurate optimization, statistics must be updated often.

2.4.2.3 Using Joins: Performance of queries can be considerably impacted by effectively crafted joins and the usage of appropriate join types (such as INNER JOIN, LEFT JOIN). Indexes on join columns that are properly organized speed up join processes.

2.4.2.4 Data Retrieval Constraints: Use SELECT statements with specified column lists and WHERE clauses to filter results to reduce the quantity of data retrieved. When only a few specific columns are required, avoid using SELECT *.

2.4.2.5 Caching: Reducing the need for repetitive database queries and speeding up response times can be achieved by caching query results or frequently requested data in memory.

2.4.2.6 Resource and Hardware Optimization: For the best database performance, you need enough CPU, RAM, and disk speed in your gear. Overall effectiveness can be increased by properly configuring the database server and allocating resources.

2.4.2.7 Continuous Maintenance: To maintain peak performance, routinely carry out database maintenance procedures like index rebuilding, rearranging, and data compaction.

2.4.2.8 Monitoring and Tuning: Utilize profiling tools and logs to continuously evaluate database performance and make necessary adjustments to resolve any performance bottlenecks.

Indexing and optimization are continual operations in database administration. A well-designed indexing approach, together with query optimization techniques, guarantees that databases can efficiently handle increasing data loads and sophisticated query needs while delivering responsive performance to consumers.

Chapter 3: SQL Syntax and Queries

3.1 SQL Syntax and Queries

SQL (Structured Query Language) is a domain-specific language used for managing and manipulating relational databases. It allows users to interact with databases by defining queries and commands to perform various operations.

Below, I'll provide an overview of SQL syntax and common types of SQL queries:

3.1.1 SQL Syntax:

3.1.1.1 SELECT Statement:

- Used to retrieve data from one or more tables.
- Syntax:

```
SELECT column1, column2, ......
FROM table_name
WHERE condition;
```

3.1.1.2 INSERT Statement:

- Used to insert new rows into a table.

```
INSERT INTO table_name (column1, column2, ......)
VALUES (value1, value2, ..........);
```

- Syntax:

3.1.1.3 UPDATE Statement:

- Used to modify existing data in a table.

```
UPDATE table_name
SET column1 = value1, column2 = value2,
..........
WHERE condition;
```

- Syntax:

3.1.1.4 DELETE Statement:

- Used to delete rows from a table.

```
DELETE FROM table_name
WHERE condition;
```

- Syntax:

Common Types of SQL Queries:

1. SELECT Queries:

- **Basic SELECT:**

```
SELECT * FROM table_name;
```

- Retrieve all columns from a table

- **Retrieve Specific Columns:**

```
SELECT column1, column2 FROM table_name;
```

- Select specific columns from a table

- **Filter data with WHERE:**

```
SELECT * FROM table_name WHERE condition ;
```

- Apply conditions to filter rows.

- **Sort Data with ORDER BY:**

```
SELECT * FROM table_name ORDER BY column1
ASC;
```

- Sort query results in ascending or descending order.

- **Aggregate Functions:**
- Perform calculations on data, such as SUM, AVG, COUNT, MAX, and MIN.

```
SELECT AVG (price) FROM products;
```

- **GROUP BY:**
- Group rows based on one or more columns for aggregate calculations.

```
SELECT category, COUNT ( * ) FROM products GROUP BY
category;
```

2. JOIN Queries:

- **INNER JOIN:**

```
SELECT orders.order_id, customers.customer_name
FROM orders
INNER JOIN customers ON orders.customer_id =
customers.customer_id;
```

- Combine rows from two or more tables on a related column.

- **LEFT JOIN (OUTER JOIN):**

```
SELECT employees.employee_name,   departments.department_name
FROM employees
LEFT JOIN departments  ON employees.department_id  =
departments.department_id;
```

- Retrieve all rows from the left table and matching rows from the right table.

3. Sub-Queries:

- Embed one query (the inner query) within another query (the outer query).

```
SELECT product_name
FROM products
WHERE category_id IN (SELECT category_id FROM categories WHERE
category_name = 'Electronics');
```

4. UPDATE and DELETE Queries:

- Modify or delete data on specific conditions.

```
UPDATE employees
SET salary = salary * 1.1
WHERE department = 'Sales';

DELETE FROM customers
WHERE last_purchase_date < '2023-01-01';
```

5. Creating and Modifying Tables:

- Create new tables and modify existing table structures.

```
CREATE TABLE employees (
        employee_id  INT PRIMARY KEY,
        first_name  VARCHAR(50),
        last_name  VARCHAR(50),
);

ALTER TABLE customers

DELETE FROM customers
        ADD COLUMN phone_number  VARCHAR(15),
```

These are only a few examples of the basic SQL syntax and query types. In relational databases, SQL is a powerful language with a wide range of features for data retrieval, modification, and management. These fundamental SQL components can be used to construct sophisticated queries and database actions.

3.2 Filtering and Sorting Data

To get particular subsets of data from a database table and present it in the correct order, SQL users frequently conduct the procedures of filtering and sorting data. The '**SELECT**' statement, coupled with the '**WHERE**' clause for filtering and the '**ORDER BY**' clause for sorting, is commonly used to carry out these actions. Here's how to use SQL to sort and filter data:

3.2.1 Utilizing the 'WHERE' clause to Filter Data

Rows from a table are filtered using the '**WHERE**' clause according to predetermined criteria. You can use it to only obtain rows that fulfil certain requirements.

```
SELECT column1, column2, ......
FROM table_name
WHERE condition;
```

3.3 Aggregation and Grouping

- **'column1, column2, ...'**: The columns you want to retrieve.
- **'table_name':** The name of the table from which **you want to retrieve data.**
- **'condition':** The condition that specifies which rows to include in the result. This condition can include comparisons, logical operators (**'AND', 'OR' 'NOT'**), and functions.

Example:

1. **Retrieve all products with a price greater than $25:**

```
SELECT product_name, price
FROM products
WHERE price > 25;
```

1. **Retrieve orders placed by a specific customer:**

```
SELECT order_id, order_date
FROM orders
WHERE customer_id = 123;
```

1. **Find employees in the "Sales" Department:**

```
SELECT employee_name,
department
FROM employees
WHERE department = 'Sales';
```

3.2.2 Sorting Data with the 'ORDER BY' Clause:

The **'ORDER BY'** clause is used to sort the result set of a query in ascending (**'ASC'**) or descending (**'DESC'**) order based on one or more columns.

```
SELECT column1, column2, .........
FROM table_name
WHERE condition
ORDER BY column1 [ASC | DESC], column2 [ASC | DESC], ......;
```

- **'column1, column2, ...'**: The columns by which you want to sort the result set.
- **'ASC'** (ascending) or **'DESC'** (descending): Specifies the sorting order. **'ASC'** is the default.

Example:

1. **Retrieve products sorted by price in descending order;**

```
SELECT product_name, price
FROM products
ORDER BY price DESC;
```

1. **Retrieve customer names sorted alphabetically.**

```
SELECT customer_name
FROM customers
ORDER BY customer_name ASC;
```

1. **Retrieve orders placed by a specific customer sorted by order date.**

```
SELECT order_id, order_date
FROM orders
WHERE customer_id = 123
ORDER BY customer_name ASC;
```

You can also combine filtering and sorting in a single query to retrieve specific subsets of data in a sorted order:

```
SELECT column1, column2, .........
FROM table_name
WHERE condition
ORDER BY column1 [ASC | DESC], column2 [ASC | DESC],
```

These SQL clauses provide flexibility in retrieving and presenting data from a database, allowing you to tailor the results to your specific requirements.

Chapter 4: Advanced SQL Concepts

4.1 Joins and Subqueries

When retrieving and modifying data from relational databases, SQL (Structured Query Language) uses the core principles of joins and subqueries. They let you to execute intricate filtering and aggregating procedures or to mix data from various tables.

An overview of SQL joins and subqueries is provided below:

4.1.1 JOINS:

Utilizing a linked column between two or more tables, a JOIN operation in SQL is used to combine rows from those tables. The **'INNER JOIN'**, **'LEFT JOIN'** (or **'LEFT OUTER JOIN'**), **'RIGHT JOIN' (or 'RIGHT OUTER JOIN')**, and **'FULL OUTER JOIN'** are the four most popular forms of joins.

Here is a quick description of each:

1. **INNER JOIN:**

- Only displays the rows with matching values across both tables.
- ***Example***: You want to include only clients who have placed orders in your list of customers and their orders.

1. **LEFT JOIN (LEFT OUTER JOIN):**

- Provides both the matched rows from the right table and all of the rows from the left table. Right table columns return NULL values if there are no matches.
- ***Example:*** An example would be retrieving a list of all employees and the projects they are allocated, even those without projects.

1. **RIGHT JOIN (RIGHT OUTER JOIN):**

- Identical to an LEFT JOIN, but returns both the matched rows from the left table and all data from the right table. NULL values are assigned to left table rows for which there are no matches.
- *Example*: You want to retrieve a list of all manufacturers, even those without any linked products, and you want to include all manufacturers.

1. **FULL OUTER JOIN:**

- When there is a match in either the left or right table, all rows are returned. Columns from the table that don't have a match are given NULL values if there are no matches.
- *Example:* To locate all customers who have placed orders and all orders, regardless of whether they have been associated, combine a list of customers and a list of orders.

4.1.2 SUBQUERIES:

A subquery is a query that is nested inside another SQL query, also referred to as a nested query or inner query. Subqueries can be used in the SELECT clause, FROM clause, WHERE clause, and HAVING clauses of a SQL statement, among other places.

Following are some typical uses for subqueries:

1. Subquery in SELECT Clause:

- Used as part of the main query to compute values or aggregate data from a related table.
- *Example:* Dividing a list of customers and orders by the average order value for each customer.

2. Subquery in WHERE Clause:

- Uses criteria derived from another table to filter rows.
- Example: Choosing personnel whose salaries are higher than the departmental average.

3. Subquery in FROM Clause:

- Assembles a temporary table or derived table that may be incorporated into the primary query.
- ***Example***: An example would be compiling a table of product sales statistics for a given time frame and then querying that data.

4. Correlated Subquery:

- A subquery that makes use of the outer query's columns in order to be run for each row that the main query processes.
- ***Example:*** Finding employees that make more than the departmental average salary, with the subquery taking department information from the outer query into account.

Subqueries are effective tools for disassembling complicated searches into more manageable chunks. Within a SQL query, they can be used to carry out operations including filtering, aggregating, and data transformation.

4.2 Views and Indexes

Views and indexes are two significant database objects in SQL that aid in streamlining and improving data processing and retrieval. Here is a description of views and indexes along with an explanation on how to utilize them:

4.2.1 VIEWS:

1. Definition: A view is a fictitious table produced by a SELECT query. It reflects a portion of data from one or more tables rather than storing any data on its own. Views give you the ability to create intricate queries, link tables, and filter data before using them to access a preset data structure just like a table.

2. Purpose:

- *Simplification*: By confining the logic and complexity within the view design, complicated queries are made simpler by views.
- *Security*: Views let you control what data users may access by limiting access to specific rows or columns.
- *Abstraction:* Views can hide the complexity of the underlying structure and give a more user- and business-friendly representation of the data.

3 Developing Views:

The SELECT query that defines a view is specified in the 'CREATE VIEW' statement when creating a view.

For Example:

```
CREATE VIEW EmployeeView AS
SELECT FirstName, LastName, Department
FROM Employees
WHERE Salary > 30000;
```

4 Querying Views:

- Once a view is created, you can query it just like a regular table using 'SELECT' statement.
- Example:

```
SELECT * FROM EmployeeView;
```

5 Updating Views:

- Depending on the database system, you may be able to update views directly, although there are limitations and considerations. Some view are read-only.
- Updates to a view can sometimes affect the underlying base tables.

4.2.2 INDEXES

1 Definition:

- An index is a database object that provides a faster way to look up data in a table. It's similar to the index in a book, which allows you to find information quickly.
- Indexes are created on one or more columns of a table and store a sorted copy of the data values along with pointers to the corresponding rows.

2 Purpose:

- *Improved Query Performance*: Indexes speed up data retrieval operations, especially for 'WHERE' clauses and 'JOIN' conditions.
- *Data Integrity*: Unique indexes ensure that column values are unique, enforcing data integrity constraints.
- *Sorting*: Indexes can help with sorting data in specific orders.

3 Creating Indexes:

- Indexes can be created using the 'CREATE INDEX' statement. The syntax varies between database systems, but it generally involves specifying the table and columns to be indexed.
- Example (for a single-column index):

```
CREATE INDEX idx_LastName ON Employees
(LastName);
```

-
-

4 Types of Indexes:

- Single-column indexes, composite indexes (indexing multiple columns), and full-text indexes (for searching text material) are examples of common index types.

- For geographic data, certain databases additionally enable spatial indexes.

5 Automatic Indexing:

- Automatic indexing is a feature of some database systems, where the database engine manages and constructs indexes based on the effectiveness of queries.

6 Index Maintenance:

- As data changes, indexes need to be kept up to date. Indexes may need to be modified in order for record addition, update, or deletion to guarantee that they continue to function properly.

7 Optimization of Query:

- Indexes are used by the database optimizer to create effective query execution plans, eliminating the requirement for full-table scans.

Views and indexes are useful resources for enhancing SQL databases. Views offer a mechanism to restrict data visibility and facilitate data access, while indexes vastly enhance query performance by enabling quick data retrieval. Database systems can be made more effective and maintained by using views and indexes properly.

4.3 Triggers and Stored Procedures

In a relational database management system (RDBMS), triggers and stored procedures are two crucial database elements that provide automation, data validation, and unique business logic. They both contribute significantly to improving data integrity, increasing productivity, and making database management simpler.

An overview of triggers and stored procedures is provided below:

4.3.1 TRIGGERS:

1. **Definition:** A trigger is a database object that, in response to a particular event or action occurring within the database, automatically executes a preset series of SQL statements (the trigger's body). Triggers can be configured to run either before or after the triggering event (for example, before an INSERT or after a UPDATE). They are event-driven.
2. **Purpose:**

- *Data Validation:* Triggers have the power to impose data integrity laws, such as verifying input, checking constraints, and preserving referential integrity.
- *Auditing:* Triggers are used to record historical records of alterations and track changes made to the data.
- *Business Logic:* They permit the execution of unique business logic, like the sending of alerts, the computation of derived values, or the carrying out of intricate transformations.

1. **Types of Triggers:**

- *Row-level Triggers:* These triggers are set off for every row that the triggering event affects.
- *Statement-level Triggers:* Regardless of the number of rows

impacted, these triggers only fire once for each triggering event.

1. **Creating Triggers:**

- Triggers are created using SQL statements within the database.
- Example (an after-insert-trigger):

```
CREATE TRIGGER AfterInsertTrigger
AFTER INSERT ON Orders
FOR EACH ROW
BEGIN
     ---- Trigger Body (SQL statement)
   INSERT INTO AuditTrail (TableName, Action,
Timestamp)
   VALUES ('Orders', 'INSERT', NOW());
END;
```

-
-

1. **Event types:**

- INSERT, UPDATE, DELETE, and database-level events like start-up and shutdown are examples of frequent events that start and stop execution.

4.3.2 STORED PROCEDURES:

1. **Definition:**

- A precompiled collection of one or more SQL statements plus procedural logic is known as a stored procedure, and it is kept in the database.
- It can be called by name and run several times with various inputs.

1. **Purpose:**

- *Code Reusability:* By encapsulating frequently used SQL logic and business actions, stored procedures support code reuse.
- *Security:* By restricting access to the data using a predetermined API, they improve security.
- *Performance:* By lowering network traffic and cutting the SQL statement compilation overhead, stored procedures can enhance query performance.

1. **Input and Output Parameters:**

- Stored procedures can accept input parameters, execute SQL statements using these parameters, and return output parameters or result sets.
- Example (a stored procedure with input and output

parameters):

```
CREATE PROCEDURE CalculateTotalPrice (
    IN productId INT
    OUT TotalPrice DECIMAL(10, 2)
)
BEGIN
  SELECT SUM(Price) INTO TotalPrice
  FROM OrderDetails
  WHERE ProductID = productId;
END;
```

-
-

1. **Creating Stored Procedures:**

- Stored procedures are typically created using SQL statements or database-specific procedural languages (e.g., PL/SQL for Oracle, T-SQL Server).
- Example (Creating a simple stored procedure):

```
CREATE PROCEDURE InsertEmployee (
      IN employeeName  VARCHAR (250),
      IN employeeSalary  DECIMAL (10, 2)
)
BEGIN
   INSERT INTO Employees (Name, Salary)
   VALUES (employeeName,  employeeSalary);
   END;
```

-
-

1. **Security and Permissions:**

- To provide granular control over data access, permissions can be applied to stored procedures apart from tables.

1. **Management of Transactions:**

- By starting, committing, or rolling back transactions as necessary, stored procedures can be used to manage transactions.

Both stored procedures and triggers have strong possibilities for improving database functionality and preserving data integrity. In contrast to stored procedures, which are called deliberately, triggers react to specified events. Your application's exact requirements and desired level of automation and control will determine which option is best for you.

4.4 Transactions and Concurrency Control

Database management systems (DBMS) depend on *transactions* and *concurrency* control to maintain data consistency and integrity in multi-user settings. They support the coordination of inserts, updates, and deletes among many concurrent database processes.

Each function can be described independently, but they are all interdependent. Users can perform many actions on the database *simultaneously* with many DBMSs. If these activities are not limited, they could conflict with one another and cause the database to break. The DBMS employs a concurrency management strategy to overcome this issue by employing a protocol that forbids database accesses from interfering with one another.

For any centralized DBMS that consists of a single database, you will learn about concurrency control and transaction support in this chapter.

An overview of transactions and concurrency control is provided below:

1. **TRANSACTIONS:**

1. **Definition:** It is a single user's or an application program's activity or series of operations that reads or modifies the database's content. A database transaction is a logical unit of work that can be a full program, a portion of a program, or a single command (such as the SQL command INSERT or UPDATE) that can involve any number of database processes. The execution of an application program can be viewed from the database's perspective as one or more transactions with interstitial non-database operations.
    - **A series of one or more database operations (SQL**

statements) is referred to as a transaction, and they are all handled as one big, indivisible unit of work.
- The ACID principles—Atomicity, Consistency, Isolation, and Durability—are observed in transactions.

2. **ACID Properties:**
   - *Autonomy:* Transactions are considered to be atomic when they are processed as a single, all-or-nothing operation. Either it completely succeeds or it completely fails.
   - *Consistency:* A transaction makes sure the database changes from a consistent state to another while maintaining data integrity restrictions.
   - *Isolation:* Transactions are kept apart from one another by isolation. Prior to the initial transaction being committed, other transactions cannot see the modifications made by the first transaction.
   - *Durability:* Once a transaction is committed, its modifications remain in effect even in the event of a system failure.
3. **Transaction States:**
   - The states of a transaction can be begin, in-progress, commit, or rollback.
   - An operation starts in the "begin" state, is carried out in the "in-progress" state, and ends with a "commit" (success) or a "rollback" (failure).
4. **Transaction Control Statements:**

Statements for managing transactions are provided by SQL:

- Starts a new transaction with the command **'BEGIN'**

'TRANSACTION' or **'START' 'TRANSACTION'**.

- **COMMIT**: Permanently commits all modifications made to a transaction.
- All changes within a transaction are undone by **'ROLLBACK'**.
- **'SAVEPOINT'**: Establishes a transactional point that can subsequently be reversed.

1. **CONCURRENCY CONTROL:**

1. Definition:

It is a technique for controlling many database processes at once without interfering with one another.

- Multiple transactions can run concurrently without violating the ACID properties thanks to concurrency control methods.
- When many transactions seek to access or edit the same data concurrently, they handle conflicts that may occur.

2. Continuity Issues:

- Lost updates, unclean reads, uncommitted data, and phantom reads are examples of common concurrency problems.
- When one transaction overwrites the modifications performed by another transaction, lost updates happen.
- A transaction reads uncommitted modifications made by another transaction when it performs a dirty read.
- Data written by a transaction but not yet committed is referred to as uncommitted data.
- When a transaction reads a group of rows that meet a requirement while a different transaction writes or deletes rows that meet the same condition, this is known as a phantom read.

3. Techniques for Concurrency Control:

- *Locking:* Locks are used to stop several transactions from simultaneously accessing or changing the same data. Exclusive locks and shared locks are typical varieties.
- *Time-Stamp based Ordering:* Transactions are given timestamps, and the DBMS makes sure that older timestamps are processed before newer ones. This is known as timestamp-based ordering.
- *Two-Phase Locking (2PL):* Transactions must adhere to a rigorous protocol specifying when locks can be obtained and released. This is known as two-phase locking (2PL).
- *Snapshot Isolation:* Each transaction starts with a consistent snapshot of the database, which is known as snapshot isolation.
- *Optimistic Concurrency Control*: Transactions move on without locks, and conflicts are found and handled at the conclusion of the transaction.

4. Levels of Isolation

Different isolation levels provided by DBMSs, including READ UNCOMMITTED, READ COMMITTED, REPEATABLE READ, and SERIALIZABLE, are used to control the level of visibility and locking in concurrent transactions.

5. Detecting Deadlocks And Breaking Them:

Deadlocks, which occur when transactions are waiting forever for each other to release locks, are detected and resolved via techniques used by DBMSs.

For maintaining data consistency and guaranteeing that several users can interact with a database concurrently without resulting in data anomalies or conflicts, effective use of transactions and concurrency management techniques is essential. Concurrency control strategy and isolation level selection should be in line with the application's particular demands and specifications.

Chapter 5: Database Administration

a. Installing and Configuring Database Systems

A crucial step in creating a database environment for your application is installing and configuring a database system. A trusted relational database management system is MySQL. With a Windows computer system, it works flawlessly. MySQL may be installed and deployed in a matter of minutes by utilizing the *MySQL Installer*, a program made to make the configuration of MySQL products simpler.

With its user-friendly interface, the MySQL Installer for Windows gives you control over the installation procedure. Additionally, it walks you through the procedures required to configure MySQL. The MySQL Installer can be downloaded by logging into your Windows server. The official website, *https://dev.mysql.com/downloads/installer*, offers a free Community edition MySQL Installer.

You have the choice of downloading the Full MySQL package or the Web Community version. The sole components of the Web version (A) are the configuration files and the MySQL Installer. Later on, you can customize and add more MySQL products. All MySQL Windows products, including the MySQL Server, are included in the Full version (B). Choose and download the version you prefer.

The general procedures for setting up a database system are as follows:

5.1.1. Decide On A Database System: Make a decision regarding the database management system (DBMS) that best fits your application. MySQL, PostgreSQL, Oracle Database, Microsoft SQL Server, MongoDB (NoSQL), and more solutions are popular choices.

5.1.2. Download Database Software: To get the installation package, go to the DBMS's official website or download page. Make sure to download the correct version for your hardware architecture (e.g., 32-bit or 64-bit) and operating system (e.g., Windows, Linux, macOS).

5.1.3. Install The Database Software: Open the installation you downloaded and run it. The steps in the installation process should be followed to specify installation directories, set up system preferences, and create an administrative user account (such as the root user for MySQL or the sysdba user for Oracle Database).

5.1.4. Configure The Database's Parameters: The majority of DBMSs have configuration files where you can specify different options, like:

- **Memory Allocation**: Set the maximum amount of RAM the database may utilize in the memory allocation.
- **Storage Paths**: Determine the locations for data files, log files, and backups in the storage paths section.
- **Network Configuration**: Select the IP addresses and ports that the database should listen on while configuring network settings.
- **Security Settings**: Configure user roles and permissions as well as authentication and authorization settings.
- **Character Encoding**: The character encoding for data storage and retrieval should be set.

Ensure that you evaluate and modify these parameters to meet the needs of your application.

5.1.5. Launch Your Database Server:

- Launch the database server once installation and

configuration are complete. Depending on the DBMS and operating system, different server start-up procedures exist.

- Common commands for starting a database server include **'sytemcrt start <service_name>'** on Linux database server. On Windows, **Windows Services Manager** is used.

5.1.6. Create Databases And Tables:

- The databases, tables, and other database objects required for your application can be created using SQL commands or a graphical database management tool.
- Using the data model for your application as a guide, define schema structures, relationships, constraints, and indexes.

5.1.7. Planning For Backup And Recovery:

- Create a backup and recovery plan to safeguard your data. Plan routine backups and test recovery processes.
- Learn how to use the tools and instructions necessary to backup and restore data.

5.1.8. Setup Connection Options:

- Set up the database driver settings or the connection string for your application to connect to the database.
- A connection pooling configuration must be made for effective database access.

5.1.9. Security And Access Management

- Put security measures in place, such as user authorization and authentication.
- Depending on user roles and permissions, limit access to

sensitive information and functions.

5.1.10. Monitoring and Performance Tuning:

- Use these techniques to monitor and optimize the performance of your database system.
- Track system health using database performance monitoring tools, spot bottlenecks, and improve queries and indexes.

5.1.11. Documentation:

- Keep thorough records that detail the database schema, configuration options, backup procedures, and recovery strategies.

5.1.12. Testing:

- To ensure data integrity, security, and performance, thoroughly test how your application interacts with the database.
- Run scalability and load tests to see how the database responds to different workloads.

5.1.13. Continuous Maintenance:

- Consistently install updates and patches to the database software to fix performance issues and resolve security flaws.
- Maintain and monitor the database to deal with problems when they occur.

A database system's installation and configuration form the basis of every application. To maintain a reliable and effective database system, it's crucial to adhere to best practices and take into account the unique requirements of your application and environment.

5.2. User Management and Access Control

Essential components of database administration include user management and access control in a database system. Data security, integrity, and compliance with privacy laws can all be ensured by effectively managing users and restricting their access to data.

The main considerations and actions for user management and access control are listed below:

5.2.1. User Roles and Privileges:

- **User Roles:** Establish user roles to classify users according to their duties and access needs. End-users, developers, and administrators are examples of typical roles.
- **Privileges:** Assign roles or certain users with certain privileges or permissions. The activities that users can take on the database, like as **SELECT, INSERT, UPDATE, DELETE**, and others, are governed by privileges.

5.2.2. User Creation and Authentication:

- **Create User Accounts**: For people who need access to the database, create user accounts. Each user ought to have their own username and strong password.
- **Authentication:** Implement robust authentication techniques, such as multi-factor authentication (MFA) and password restrictions (complexity, expiration, etc.), to increase security.

5.2.3. Access Control and Authorization:

- **Authorisation Rules:** To control which users or roles can access particular database objects (tables, views, procedures, etc.), establish authorization rules.
- **Row-Level Security:** Consider using row-level security to limit user access to particular rows inside a table depending on specified conditions or requirements.

5.2.4. Permission Award and Withdrawal:

- **GRANT Statements**: To grant rights to users or roles, use SQL GRANT statements. For example: '**GRANT SELECT ON'** 'table_name' **TO** 'user_name';
- **REVOKE Statements:** Use SQL REVOKE statements to revoke previously given rights, if necessary.

5.2.5. Monitoring and Auditing:

- **Audit Trails:** Using audit trails, you can keep track of user activity and keep track of who visited the database, what they did, and when they did it.
- **Monitoring Tools:** Use monitoring tools and database logs to track database access continually and spot any illegal or suspicious activity.

5.2.6. Encryption Of Databases:

- **Data Encryption:** Encrypt your data both in transit and at rest to prevent unauthorized access to sensitive information. Use Transparent Data Encryption (TDE) for data at rest and SSL/TLS for data in transit.

5.2.7. Management of Sessions and Temporary Access

- **Temporary Access:** Create user accounts for temporary access that have short lifespans and rights that expire after they are no longer required.
- **Session Management:** Implement session management to control the duration and termination of user sessions.

5.2.8. Regulations For Compliance And Privacy:

- **Compliance:** Ensure that your user management and access control procedures comply with organizational policies as well as industry standards (such as GDPR and HIPAA).

5.2.9. Regular Evaluations and Audits:

- **User Reviews:** To make sure that access control is current and in compliance with security policies, periodically examine user accounts, privileges, and access logs.
- **Access Audits:** Auditing access control settings and conducting security assessments to find weaknesses and areas for development.

5.2.10. Backup And Disaster Recovery:

- **Backup User Information**: When creating database backups and disaster recovery plans, remember to include user account details, role assignments, and access control settings.

5.2.11. Documentation:

- **User Documentations:** Keep records of user accounts, roles, and access control regulations. Authorized personnel should have simple access to this documentation.

5.2.12. Training and Education

- **User Education**: Educate users on security best practices, such as password security and data access guidelines.

Access control and user management are essential elements of a strong database security approach. You can assist in preventing unwanted access to your data, lowering security risks, and ensuring regulatory compliance by putting these measures into effect. Your access control policies should be reviewed and updated frequently to reflect evolving security requirements and threats.

5.3. Backup and Recovery Strategies

In order to protect data integrity and guarantee business continuity in the case of data loss or system failures, it is essential to implement reliable backup and recovery techniques. The essential elements and recommended techniques for developing backup and recovery plans for a database system are listed below:

5.3.1. Specify Recovery Objectives:

- Establish precise recovery goals, such as recovery time and point objectives (RTO and RPO). RTO and RPO both specify the allowable downtime and the acceptable data loss, respectively.

5.3.2. Pick the Right Backup Types:

- **Full Backups:** Take a snapshot of the entire database at a certain time. The database is completely captured in full backups.
- **Differential Backups:** Archive database modifications made since the last complete backup. Compared to full backups, these backups are easier to produce and restore.
- **Incremental Backup**: Save modifications made since the last backup, which could have been a complete or incremental backup. Although they may take longer to restore, incremental backups are effective in terms of storage.

5.3.3. Schedule Regular Backups:

- Create backup plans depending on the RPO and RTO specifications. Daily full backups and more frequent differential or incremental backups throughout the day are examples of frequent backups.

5.3.4. Redundant And Off-Site Storage:

- To safeguard against natural disasters like fires or floods, save backup copies in a safe place that is not on-site.
- Reduce the risk of data loss due to hardware failures by implementing redundancy by storing backups on many media types (such as tape, disk, and the cloud).

5.3.5. Backup verification:

- Make regular tests of the backups' integrity by restoring them to a different setting. By doing this, backups are made to be reliable and successful when restored.

5.3.6. Implement Retention Policies:

- Create data retention guidelines to control the backup lifecycle. Set a time limit on how long backups should be kept before being archived or deleted.

5.3.7. Utilize Incremental and Transaction Log Backups:

- Implement frequent transaction log backups for databases that require little data loss. Changes since the last transaction log backup are included in these backups.
- To achieve both RTO and RPO goals, think about combining complete, differential, and transaction log backups.

5.3.8. Checks for Database Consistency:

- Conduct regular database consistency checks to find and fix any problems in the database before they have an influence on backups.

5.3.9. Plan for Disaster Recovery:

- Create a thorough disaster recovery strategy that lays out what you do in the case of a significant data loss or system failure. Incorporate roles and duties, communication procedures, and the order of events into the plan.

5.3.10. Backup Encryption:

- To safeguard critical data during storage and transfer, encrypt backup files.

5.3.11. Monitor Backup Jobs

- Keep an eye out for any irregularities or failures in backup jobs. Create alerting systems to inform administrators of backup problems.

5.3.12. Version Control and documentation

- Ensure that backup and recovery procedures are documented, along with backup schedules, retention guidelines, and recovery goals.

5.3.13. Training for Staff:

- In order to ensure that database administrators and IT employees can react appropriately during major incidents, train them on backup and recovery processes.

5.3.14. Regular Testing:

- Test your recovery methods on a regular basis to make sure they work by simulating actual situations.

5.3.15. Vendor Support:

- Be knowledgeable about the recommended practices for your database system and vendor-specific backup and recovery options. Utilize the resources for vendor support as necessary.

A thorough data security and disaster recovery plan must include a well-designed backup and recovery method. It makes sure that in the event of unforeseen circumstances or disasters, your firm can recover from data loss incidents, reduce downtime, and retain data integrity.

5.4 Monitoring and Performance Tuning

To make sure that your database system operates effectively, performs well, and satisfies the requirements of your application, monitoring and performance tweaking are essential components of database administration. The following are the essential elements and recommended practices for performance monitoring in a database environment:

1. **Establish Baselines:** Create baseline performance metrics for your database system to get started. These measurements could include things like query response times, disk I/O, CPU utilization, and memory usage.
2. **Use Database Monitoring Tools:** Implement database monitoring programs and technologies that offer on-the-fly analyses of your database's performance. Prometheus, Grafana, SQL Server Profiler, and Oracle Enterprise Manager are well-known database monitoring tools.
3. **Track Important Metrics:**

Keep track of important database metrics, such as:

- CPU and memory utilisation
- Disk I/O and latency
- Query execution times and bottlenecks
- Counts for connections and sessions
- Issues with locking and blocking
- Cache hit rates (for example, query cache and buffer cache)
- Query optimization and query execution plans
    1. **Alert and Notifications:**

- Create alerting systems so you can be informed when specific performance criteria are crossed. You can respond swiftly to problems before they affect users with the aid of alerts.

1. **Query Optimisation:**

- Review and refine database queries and execution strategies frequently to enhance query performance. To find slow-moving queries, use tools like query analysers and database profiling.

1. **Indexing Technique:**

- To speed up data retrieval, make sure your database tables contain the right indexes. Avoid over-indexing, though, as this can cause performance issues when updating data.

1. **Data Archiving and Purging:**

- Utilize data cleansing and archiving techniques to delete or archive unnecessary data, thereby lowering table size and enhancing query performance.

1. **Hardware Upgrades:**

- To address performance constraints, take into account hardware upgrades like adding more RAM, quicker storage devices (like SSDs), or additional CPUs.

1. **Query Caching:**

- If your database system supports it, employ query caching technologies to save and reuse frequently used queries and their results.

1. **Connection Pooling:**

- Reduce the overhead of connection construction and teardown by using connection pooling to effectively manage and reuse database connections.

1. **Database Tuning parameters**:

- To maximize performance, modify database configuration parameters (such as buffer pool size and query cache size) in accordance with resource availability and workload.

1. **Monitor Long-Running Transactions:**

- Find and fix persistent transactions that can obstruct other transactions and have an impact on database performance.

1. **Schedules for backup and maintenance**

- To avoid interfering with user activities, plan and schedule database backup and maintenance tasks for times when there is little activity.

1. **Load Balancing And High Availability**

- Distribute traffic and assure system availability by putting high availability solutions (such load balancing, replication, and clustering) into place.

1. **Security And Access Management**

- To identify and stop unwanted access or data breaches, constantly monitor security settings and access limits.

1. **Regular Performance Testing:**

- To determine the database's capacity to handle additional loads and to spot any bottlenecks, do routine load and performance testing.

1. **Knowledge Sharing And Documentation**

- Keep track of your performance tuning efforts, best practices, and learnings. To collaboratively improve database administration, share information within your team.

1. **Planning For Capacity:**

- To make sure that your database system can handle growing data volumes and user loads, estimate future growth and capacity demands.

1. **Continuous Improvement:**

- Consider performance tweaking to be a continuous activity. Analyse and improve the database continuously to adjust to shifting usage patterns and requirements.

Maintaining a robust and responsive database system requires effective monitoring and performance optimization procedures. By regularly monitoring and improving your database's performance, you can make sure that it can scale, deliver reliable response times, and satisfy user and application demands.

Chapter 6: Data Warehousing and Business Intelligence

6.1 Data Warehousing Concepts

Modern corporate intelligence and data management need the use of data warehousing. In order to enhance business decision-making, it entails the process of gathering, storing, and managing data from numerous sources.

You need to have a firm grasp of data warehousing and business intelligence (BI) technologies in order to use analytics to achieve progressive digital transformation. You must also realize that they are more than just platforms because they are the gateways to insight and strategic choice-making for your company. In order to make judgments about how your company is interacting with and influencing its audience, governed data curation may fill the gap between raw data collected purely for the purpose of statistics and data storytelling, a new language.

1. **Definition of Data Warehousing?**

Data from numerous sources is gathered and stored in a data warehouse. Similar to saving files or pictures on the cloud, housing or storing the material in a digital "warehouse" It is simpler to use and yields more insights when you have a place to keep your data on a greater scale. To report the most recent and integrated data, you can import historical data or timely data sources. A data warehouse can be used for commercial reporting and analytical reasons. You should nevertheless develop an integrated data strategy and an accurate audience story if you want to fully utilize all of your data. Our advice is to integrate your data warehouse with the rest of your business intelligence procedures.

1. **Definition of Business Intelligence?**

Most people refer to the platforms and procedures for the gathering, integrating, analysing, and presenting of business information when they use the phrase "business intelligence" or "BI." However, BI goes beyond that; it improves company decision-making by ensuring that choices are strategic. With BI, you have data to support why, based on prior performance and study, one solution would be more effective than another.

1. **How does Data warehousing and Business Intelligence collaborate?**

Although they both function in the same area, business intelligence and data warehousing are fundamentally different concepts. Data warehouses and business intelligence both include data storage. However, data collection, technique, and analysis are all part of business intelligence. A data warehouse, on the other hand, is primarily the organization and storage of such data in order to support BI activities. The upkeep and deployment of a data warehouse are so essential to business intelligence (BI) that they are frequently referred to as Business Intelligence – Data Warehousing (BI-DW).

The loading time for compiling and analysing data can be sped up with an effective data warehouse. Additionally, it can enhance data security, data compliance, storage capability, integration compatibility, and data sharing. Therefore, the appropriate business intelligence utilizing the correct data in your data warehouse enables numerous techniques that can support strategic decision-making.

The following are some essential ideas and elements in data warehousing:

1. **Data Warehouse:**

- A data warehouse is a central location where structured, organized data from diverse sources is kept.

- It is made to aid in data analysis, reporting, and decision-making for business.

    1. **Data Integration**

- Data extraction from various sources, format conversion, and data warehouse loading are all steps in the data integration process.
- In order to integrate data, a common technique is called ETL (Extract, Transform, and Load).

    1. **Data Mart**

- A data mart is a portion of a data warehouse that is concentrated on a certain division or function of business.
- To offer more specialized and department-specific views of data, data marts are frequently employed.

    1. **Dimensional Modelling**:

- Data warehousing employs the data modelling method known as dimensional modelling.
- Facts (quantifiable business measures) and dimensions (contextual factors that define the facts) are used to organize the data.
- Common dimensional modelling techniques include the star and snowflake schemas.

    1. **Data Purging:**

- Prior to being placed into the data warehouse, flaws or inconsistencies in the data are found and corrected through the process of "data cleansing."
- This guarantees the reliability and accuracy of the data.

1. **Data Warehouses Architecture:**

A variety of architectural models can be used to construct data warehouses, including:

- **Single-Tier**: A single repository is used to store data.
- **Two-Tier**: Data is divided into databases for reporting and operations.
- **Three-Tier**: Data is separated into three layers: extraction, transformation, and loading.

1. **Schema for Data Warehouses:**

- The data warehouse's data structure is specified by the schema.
- Star schema, snowflake schema, and galaxy schema are examples of typical schema types.

1. **Tools for Data Warehouses:**

- The utilization of database management systems (DBMS), ETL tools, reporting and analytics tools, and data visualization tools are only a few of the technologies and tools utilized in data warehousing.

1. **Performance Tuning For Data Warehouses:**

- To guarantee that queries on the data warehouse operate effectively, performance optimization is essential.
- Indexing, partitioning, and query execution plan optimization are examples of techniques.

1. **Best Practices for Data Warehouses:**

- For data warehousing to be successful, best practices, such as data governance, data quality management, and security, must be followed.

1. **Data Warehousing Challenges**

- Complexities in data integration, handling enormous amounts of data, assuring data quality, and adjusting to shifting business requirements are some of the common problems.

1. **Data Warehousing In the Cloud:**

- Cloud-based data warehousing solutions, which provide scalability, flexibility, and cost-efficiency, are increasingly being used by many enterprises.

1. **Security for Data Warehouses:**

- It is crucial to protect the data in the data warehouse. Access control, encryption, and auditing are security mechanisms.

1. **Automation of Data Warehouses:**

- The entire data warehousing process, from ETL to schema creation and maintenance, can be streamlined using automation technologies.

1. **Trends in Data Warehousing**

- Data warehousing trends include the utilization of real-time data, big data technology, and machine learning and artificial intelligence integration.

For enterprises to effectively use their data for business insights and decision-making, data warehousing is a need. It is essential in today's data-driven businesses.

6.2 ETL (Extract, Transform, Load) Processes

Data integration and warehousing are fundamentally based on the ETL (Extract, Transform, and Load) process. For analysis and reporting, it entails moving and transforming data from source systems into a data warehouse or other target systems.

Thus, the data integration process known as ETL, or extract, transform, and load, brings together data from several data sources into a single, consistent data store that is then loaded into a data warehouse or other destination system. ETL, a procedure for integrating and loading data for computation and analysis, was established as databases gained popularity in the 1970s. Eventually, it became the main way to process data for data warehousing projects.

Workstreams in data analytics and machine learning are built on the basis provided by ETL. ETL cleans and arranges data through a set of business rules in a way that satisfies particular business intelligence requirements, such monthly reporting, but it can also handle more advanced analytics that might enhance back-end operations or end-user experiences.

ETL is frequently used by a company to:

- Extract information from old systems
- Cleanse the data to increase its uniformity and quality.
- Insert data into the desired database.

Here is a summary of the ETL process and its essential elements:

6.2.1. Extract:

- **Data Extraction**: Data is extracted during this stage from a variety of source systems, including databases, flat files, APIs, web services, and more. Real-time or batch extraction techniques are both possible.

- **Data Profiling**: Data profiling is the process of studying the structure, quality, and relationships of the source data. It aids in identifying problems with data quality and the need for data transformation.

6.2.2. Transform:

- **Data Transformation:** To fulfil the needs of the destination system, data from the source systems frequently has to be changed. Data cleansing, validation, aggregation, normalization, and enrichment are some of the tasks involved in transformation.
- **Data Mapping**: Data mapping describes the correspondence between the data pieces in the source and target systems. Based on these mappings, transformation rules are implemented.
- **Business Rules:** To guarantee data consistency and integrity, business rules are enforced during transformation. Data validation, computations, and data enrichment can all be handled by these rules.
- **Data Quality Checks**: Data anomalies, errors, and missing values are found and handled using data quality checks. Data accuracy is maintained via quality checks.

6.2.3. Load:

- **Data Loading:** During this stage, the transformed data is put into the desired analytical database, data warehouse, or data mart. There are several methods for loading, including bulk loading, incremental loading, and real-time streaming.
- **Indexing:** To enhance query performance in the destination system, indexes may be formed on the loaded data.

- **Logging and Auditing:** Mechanisms for logging and auditing are frequently implemented to keep track of the ETL process, keep track of data lineage, and guarantee data governance.
- **Error Handling:** Mechanisms are in place to collect, log, and manage any faults that may arise during the loading process. Retrying failed records is an option, as is sending them to an error handling queue for human review.

6.2.4. Management of Metadata:

- Data about data, or metadata, is a critical component of ETL procedures. It contains details on the data lineage, transformations, mappings, and source data.
- Understanding data flow, keeping track of changes, and maintaining data lineage are all critical for data governance and compliance thanks to metadata management.

6.2.5. Dependence management:

- ETL procedures frequently rely on other ETL tasks and the availability of the source data. Dependency management makes sure that tasks are completed in the proper order and that the necessary data is available prior to processing.

6.2.6. Optimizing Performance Through Monitoring

- To guarantee data quality, performance, and reliability, ETL procedures must be continuously monitored. Techniques for performance optimization may include query tweaking, caching, and parallel processing.

6.2.7. Automation and Scalability

- ETL procedures must to be scalable to handle increasing data quantities. ETL tasks are streamlined and require less manual involvement thanks to automation tools and workflows.

6.2.8. Error Handling and Recovery:

- To ensure that ETL operations can recover gracefully from failures without data loss or corruption, robust error handling and recovery procedures are essential.

In a data warehousing context, ETL processes are essential for preserving the quality and consistency of data. They give businesses the ability to turn basic data into insightful information that can be used for reporting and decision-making.

6.3. OLAP (Online Analytical Processing)

A type of computer processing known as OLAP (Online Analytical Processing) permits interactive study of massive amounts of data from various angles. For complicated and multidimensional data processing, it's an essential piece of technology utilized in business intelligence and data warehousing systems. Users of OLAP systems can explore and analyse data in a way that helps them make decisions.

You can use software called online analytical processing (OLAP) to evaluate business data from many angles. Data is gathered and stored by organizations from a variety of sources, including internal systems, smart meters, websites, and applications. This data is combined and organized into categories using OLAP to produce insights that may be used in strategic planning. For instance, a retailer might keep information about every item it sells, including the colour, size, price, and location.

In a distinct method, the merchant additionally gathers information about consumer purchases, such as the names of the items ordered and the total sales amount. To address issues like whether product colours are more in demand or how product placement affects sales, OLAP mixes the databases.

6.3.1. Why is OLAP Crucial?

Organizations can process and profit from an increasing amount of digital information with the use of online analytical processing (OLAP). The following are a few advantages of OLAP:

- **View of Integrated Data:** For business units like marketing, finance, production, and others, OLAP offers a single platform. Managers and decision-makers are able to solve issues by looking at the wider picture. They can carry out what-if analysis, which illustrates how actions made by one department affect various parts of the company.

- **Accelerated Decision-Making:** In order to stay competitive in a quick-paced industry, businesses use OLAP to make prompt and precise judgments. The computer system must search through numerous data tables when running analytical queries on multiple relational databases. However, OLAP systems pre-calculate and integrate data so that business analysts can produce reports more quickly when they are required.
- **Support for Non-Technical Users:** Complex data analysis is made simpler for non-technical business users by OLAP solutions. Instead of learning how to use databases, business users can create complicated analytical calculations and generate reports.

These are the main OLAP ideas and characteristics:

1. **Model for Multidimensional Data:**

- Data is arranged into a multidimensional model in OLAP, which is frequently referred to as a "cube." Data are represented by this model as dimensions and measures.
- Data can be sliced and diced according to dimensions, which are traits or characteristics. Examples of common dimensions are time, region, product, and customer. The numerical data points that are being studied are called measures, for example, sales revenue, profits, or quantities sold.

    1. **Hypercubes and Cuboids**:

- A cuboid is a more compact variation of the larger data cube. It stands for a certain set of dimensions and measurements.
- The entire data cube, including all conceivable dimensions and measurements, is referred to as a hypercube.

1. **Operation of OLAP:**

Numerous processes for data analysis are supported by OLAP systems, including:

- **Slicing:** Choosing just one dimension to display a specific cross-section of the data cube is known as "slicing."
- **Dicing:** Choosing two or more dimensions to examine a subcube via dicing.
- **Pivoting (Rotation):** Change the cube's orientation to examine data from various angles by pivoting (rotating).
- **Drill-Down and Roll-Up**: Using hierarchy levels inside dimensions to move between views of the data at various granularities.
- **Aggregation:** Summarizing data at more abstract levels (e.g., annual total sales).
- **Calculations:** Making calculations for measurements, such as figuring out growth rates or market shares.

1. **Types of OLAP**

OLAP systems can be divided into various sorts according to their design and method of data storage:

- **MOLAP (Multidimensional OLAP):** Data is kept in multidimensional cubes and processed using specific MOLAP databases, such as Microsoft Analysis Services and IBM Cognos TM1.
- **ROLAP** (Relational OLAP): OLAP capability is implemented using SQL queries, and data is stored in relational databases (e.g., Oracle OLAP, SAP BW).
- **HOLAP (Hybrid OLAP):** Combining MOLAP and ROLAP, offers the benefits of both methodologies (for example, Microsoft SQL Server Analysis Services).

- **DOLAP (Desktop OLAP):** OLAP capability is made available to users directly on their desktops, eliminating the requirement for a separate server (example: Excel PivotTables).

1. **Performance Enhancement:**

- With capabilities like caching, indexing, and pre-aggregation to guarantee quick query responses, OLAP systems are built for performance.
- To enhance query performance, data is frequently aggregated at various granularity levels.

1. **Data Reporting and Visualization:**

- To build interactive dashboards and reports, OLAP systems are frequently connected with data visualization programs and reporting frameworks.
- Users can develop unique reports based on their findings and visually explore the data.

1. **Business Applications:**

- Numerous business applications, such as financial analysis, sales forecasting, customer segmentation, inventory management, and others, frequently employ OLAP.
- It aids in the discovery of patterns, anomalies, and insights in data and supports complicated ad hoc queries.

By offering a flexible and dynamic way to evaluate and explore data, OLAP technology plays a crucial role in assisting enterprises in making wise decisions. Modern business intelligence and data analytics technologies are built on this fundamental principle.

6.4 Reporting and Data Visualization

Reporting and data visualization are both methods for presenting data, although they each use a distinct approach. Reporting is highly chaotic because it delivers the facts in a thorough manner that is challenging to absorb; for this reason, data visualization is regarded as the best. Since it merely makes the material easier to absorb, the convenience it offers by turning the information into pictures benefits in many ways.

Data analytics and business intelligence (BI) both depend on reporting and data visualization. To aid in decision-making and offer insights, they entail presenting data in an appealing and clear manner.

The following are important ideas and best practices in reporting and data visualization:

6.4.1 REPORTING: Reporting is the process of creating organized data that is frequently tabular or textual and summarizes and shows facts in a consistent manner. Typically, reports are intended to communicate specific data findings or trends.

Business reporting, often known as "enterprise reporting," refers to both "the public reporting of cost and revenue data by a business company" and "the routine supply of services to decision-makers inside an organization to assist them in their job." It plays a significant role in a larger effort to improve corporate intelligence and information management.

With a database system, extract, convert, and load (ETL) techniques are frequently utilized, then one or more reporting approaches. Reports can be downloaded from a company's website, printed out, or sent through email. The creation of consolidated reports, which include diverse organizational views, has expanded with the advent of information technology. Consolidated reports, which compile diverse viewpoints of an entity in one place, have become more common as a result of advancements in information technology. This reporting process needs searching information sources using multiple logical templates in order to produce a text that can be read by humans.

6.4.1.1 Reporting Formats:

- **Operational Reports:** These include the daily information required for typical corporate operations.
- **Ad-hoc Reports**: Users can produce these reports as needed to address certain inquiries.
- **Analytical Reports:** These are used for in-depth examination and frequently include graphs and charts.
- **Dashboards:** Dashboards are visual representations of metrics and key performance indicators (KPIs) that give quick insights into how well a business is performing.

1. **Report Layout:**

- The three pillars of effective report design are relevancy, simplicity, and clarity.
- When developing reports, take the readership and their needs into account.
- Formatting, titles, and labels should all be consistent.

1. **Sources Of Data**

- Data from spreadsheets, databases, data warehouses, and external APIs are all gathered for reports.
- Ensure the quality, consistency, and accuracy of the data.

1. **Automation:**

- Set up a schedule and automate the creation of reports to guarantee timely and reliable delivery.
- Use automation and distribution-supporting reporting technologies.

1. **Interactivity:**

- Users can apply filters to data or drill down for more specifics in some reports to engage with the data.

6.4.2 DATA VISUALIZATION

- Data visualization is the act of transforming large amounts of information that are difficult to remember into visualizations like graphs, charts, patterns, etc. This procedure is carried out to make it simple to study and comprehend that volume of data.

Humans are more adaptable to pictures than they are to textual documents; their eyes are better at catching images. To effectively and efficiently communicate information, data visualization employs statistical visuals, charts, database graphics, and other techniques. Numerical Data can be encrypted utilizing Dots, Lines, or Bars to Graph a Statistical Message.

A strong visualization can help users interpret and debate facts and data. Complex data is more easily accessible, understandable, and usable as a result. The graphical display of data for the purpose of assisting users in understanding patterns, trends, and insights is known as data visualization. It improves accessibility and actionability of complex data.

6.4.2.1 Types of Data Visualizations

- **Chat and Graphs:** Bar charts, line charts, pie charts, scatter plots, and heat maps are examples of common graphs and charts.
- **Tables**: For showing detailed facts, well-structured tables might be useful.
- **Maps:** Maps can be used to visualize geographic data.

- **Infographics:** These display information by fusing text, pictures, and other visual elements.

6.4.2.2 Selecting the Proper Visualization

- Choose a visualization type that best conveys the data and your intended message.
- Think about how familiar the audience is with various chart types.

6.4.2.3 Colour and Design:

- To improve aesthetic appeal, regularly use colours, typefaces, and styling.
- Consider your colour choices with regard to accessibility.

1. **Storytelling:**

- A story or a message should be told through data visualization.
- Make use of headings, captions, and labels to lead the audience through the story.

1. **Interactivity:**

- Users can study data in an interactive visualization at their own pace.
- Tooltips, zooming, filtering, and animations are all forms of interaction.

1. **Data Preparation:**

- Before developing visualizations, data must be properly cleaned, prepared, and organized.
- When working with huge datasets, take data aggregation and summarization into consideration.

1. **Platforms and Tools**

- For data visualization, a variety of tools and platforms are available, including Tableau, Power BI, D3.js, and Excel.
- Pick a tool that fits the requirements and expertise of your firm.

6.4.2.8 Accessibility:

- By using alternative text and other accessibility elements, make sure people with disabilities can access visualizations.

Making educated decisions and releasing the value of data depend on effective reporting and data visualization. They give businesses a way to share knowledge and encourage action based on data-driven information.

Chapter 7: NoSQL Databases and New Database Paradigms

7.1 Introduction to NoSQL Databases

NoSQL databases are a class of database management systems created to store and retrieve data that doesn't cleanly fit into the conventional relational database architecture. They are also known as "Not Only SQL" databases. These databases offer relational databases versatile and scalable substitutes for managing massive amounts of unstructured, semi-structured, or dynamically changing data.

Managing and manipulating large volumes of information has become essential in today's data-driven environment. The standard method for storing and accessing structured data has long been traditional SQL (Structured Query Language) databases. However, the need for more adaptable and scalable solutions has risen as the size and complexity of data have increased. We now have NoSQL databases, a paradigm that questions the strict SQL structures and offers novel options for data storage and retrieval.

The term "Not Only SQL," or NoSQL, was created to characterize a variety of database systems that are different from the conventional relational databases built on SQL. Modern applications generate enormous amounts of unstructured, semi-structured, and dynamically changing data, which NoSQL databases are made to handle. NoSQL databases offer a flexible and schema-less method of data storing, in contrast to SQL databases that follow a specified structure.

Here is a summary of NoSQL databases:

7.1.1. Important Features of NoSQL Databases

- **Schema-Less:** NoSQL databases are frequently schema-less, which means that no predetermined schema is necessary for the data to be stored in them. This enables flexible and dynamic data modelling.
- **Flexible Data Models:** They are compatible with a wide range of data models, including document-based (MongoDB,

for example), key-value (Redis), column-family (Apache Cassandra, for example), and graph-based (Neo4j). Each model is appropriate for various data kinds and application situations.

- **Scalability:** A lot of NoSQL databases are made to be horizontally scalable, which enables them to handle enormous amounts of data and significant traffic loads. They are easily scalable across numerous nodes or servers.
- **High Performance:** NoSQL databases can provide excellent read and write performance since they are tailored for certain use cases. This is especially advantageous for applications that need real-time functionality.
- **Non-Relational:** Unlike conventional relational databases, which use tables with rows and columns to store data, NoSQL databases do not. They make use of different storage methods, which are frequently better for particular kinds of data.
- **Consistent Models:** Strong consistency, eventual consistency, and customizable consistency are some of the several consistency models that NoSQL databases frequently provide. This enables developers to select the degree of data consistency that best matches the needs of their application.

7.1.2. Different NoSQL Database Types

- **Document-Based Databases:** Databases that store data in flexible, semi-structured documents (like JSON or XML) are known as document-based databases. CouchDB and MongoDB are two examples.
- **Key-Value Stores:** These databases keep information in key-value pairs, enabling caching and straightforward data retrieval. Examples include Amazon DynamoDB and Redis.
- **Column-Family Stores:** Instead of organizing data into tables, column-family databases group data into families of

columns, which can offer great write and read scalability. HBase and Apache Cassandra are two examples.

- **Graph Databases:** These are perfect for querying and traversing relationships in data because they are made to represent and store data in a graph-like structure. Amazon Neptune and Neo4j are two examples.
- **Time-Series Databases:** These are frequently used for IoT and monitoring applications because they are well-suited for processing time-stamped data. Prometheus and InfluxDB are two examples.

7.1.3. Examples of NoSQL databases in Use:

- **Big Data:** NoSQL databases are well suited for managing the enormous volumes of data produced by big data applications.
- **Real-Time Analytics:** They perform well in situations needing quick access to data and immediate processing.
- **Content Management:** NoSQL databases are frequently used by content management systems to handle a variety of unstructured content.
- **Internet of Things (IoT):** NoSQL databases can effectively store and analyse the enormous amount of data produced by Internet of Things (IoT) devices.
- **Personalization and User Profiles:** They are used to store behavioural information and user profiles for application personalization.
- **Caching:** To enhance application performance, frequently accessed data is cached in key-value stores like Redis.

When data structures are dynamic, the scale is large, or performance demands are stringent, NoSQL databases offer a useful alternative to conventional relational databases. But selecting the ideal NoSQL database for a given use case necessitates giving significant thought to the data model, consistency specifications, and scalability considerations.

7.2 Types of NoSQL Databases (Document, Key-Value, Column-family, Graph)

There are different types of NoSQL databases, each created to meet a particular purpose for data storage and retrieval. Document-based, Key-Value stores, Column-family stores, and Graph databases are the four main categories of NoSQL databases.

Non-relational databases don't have as strict of a database schema as relational databases, which organize data in a tabular format. In actuality, depending on the type of database, non-relational databases structure data differently. Regardless of the kind of non-relational database, they all try to address the problems of relational models' rigidity and scalability that make them unsuitable for unstructured data forms like text, video, and photos.

Here is a description of each kind:

1. **Document-Based Databases:** Document databases, as the name suggests, store data as documents. Data are often saved in JSON, XML, or BSON formats, and they can be useful for managing semi-structured data. As a result, less translation is required to use the data in applications because the data is kept together. Since data formats do not have to match across documents (for example, name vs. Last_name), developers also have more flexibility. However, this can cause data corruption in transactions that are sophisticated. User profiles and content management systems are common applications for document databases. MongoDB, the MEAN stack's database, is an illustration of a document-oriented database.

- **What they Store:** Data is stored in flexible, semi-structured documents using document-based databases. Typically, these documents are in XML, JSON, or BSON (Binary JSON) forms.

- **Use Cases**: Applications where data is hierarchical and varies from one record to another are well-suited for document-based databases. User profiles, e-commerce platforms, and content management systems are examples of typical use cases.
- **Examples:** MongoDB, CouchDB, RavenDB, and Firebase Firestore are a few examples.

1. **Key-Value Stores:** Each item in this dictionary of key-value pairs, which is the structure of this schema-free data model, has a key and a value. The value is an array of data, such as each individual item in that user's shopping cart, whereas the key may be akin to something like a shopping cart ID found in a SQL database. It is frequently used for caching and storing user session data, such shopping cart information. When you need to fetch several records at once, it's less than ideal. Examples of open-source databases that use this data model are Redis and Memcached.

- **What they Store:** Data is stored in key-value stores as straightforward key-value pairs, where each value is matched with a distinct key. Values might range from straightforward strings to intricate data structures.
- **Use Cases**: When quick and easy data retrieval is essential, key-value storage shine. They are frequently employed for data handling, session management, and caching.
- **Examples**: Redis, Amazon DynamoDB, Riak, and Berkeley DB are a few examples.

1. **Wide-Column Store:** These databases organize data into columns, allowing users to access only the ones

they need without using extra RAM for unnecessary information. Although this database attempts to address the drawbacks of key-value and document stores, it is not advised for usage by fresher teams and projects because of how difficult it may be to administer. A couple of examples of open-source, wide-column databases are Apache HBase and Apache Cassandra. The Hadoop Distributed Files System, which offers a method of storing sparse data sets and is frequently utilized in many big data applications, is the foundation upon which Apache HBase is constructed. The opposite is true for Apache Cassandra, which was created to manage massive volumes of data across several servers and clustering that spans numerous data centres. It has been applied to many different use cases, including real-time data analytics and social networking websites.

- **What they Store**: Data is organized into column families using column-family stores, which have a more flexible schema than relational databases' tables. A different set of columns may be present in each column family.
- **Use Cases**: Applications that demand high write and read scalability should use column-family storage. They are frequently employed in analytics, monitoring systems, and time-series data storage.
- **Examples** include Amazon SimpleDB, HBase, ScyllaDB, and Apache Cassandra.

1. **Graph Databases:** Data from a knowledge graph is often stored in this kind of database. Nodes, edges, and properties are the storage types for data

elements. A node can be anything, location, or person. The connection between the nodes is described by an edge. The management and storage of a graph's network of connections between its pieces is done using graph databases. Neo4j is a graph-based database service built on Java that comes in both a pre-packaged licensed version with backup and extensions included and an open-source community edition where users can buy licenses for online backup and high availability extensions.

- **What They Store:** Data is represented and stored using a graph-like structure made up of nodes, edges, and properties in graph databases. They are experts in analysing data correlations and modelling them.
- **Use Cases**: Complex relationship-based applications like social networks, recommendation systems, fraud detection, and network analysis need the use of graph databases.
- **Examples**: Neo4j, Amazon Neptune, OrientDB, and ArangoDB are a few examples.

Every NoSQL database type has been tailored for particular use cases and data structures. The requirements of your application, the data structure, the need for scalability, and the query patterns all play a role in selecting the best NoSQL database. For diverse data processing and storage requirements within the same system, current applications frequently combine NoSQL databases and conventional relational databases.

Additionally, suffice to note that NoSQL databases favour availability over consistency. Computers that operate across a network must always choose between giving users consistent results (where every response is the same) and high availability, sometimes known as "availability." The "CAP Theory," which stands for Consistency,

Availability, or Partition Tolerance, is what this is. Relational databases make sure the data is constantly consistent and in sync. Redis is one NoSQL database that prefers to always respond.

This means that the results of a query could be off by a few seconds, possibly even a minute. This results in users on social networking platforms seeing an outdated profile photo while the most recent one is only a few seconds ago. An error or timeout could be an alternative. However, in banking and financial activities, a mistake and resubmission could be preferable to outdated, inaccurate information.

7.3 Use Cases for NoSQL Databases

NoSQL databases are a useful resource for dealing with particular use cases when conventional relational databases might not be the best option. NoSQL databases are more adaptable, scalable, and performant when dealing with unstructured, semi-structured, or dynamically changing data. Here are a few frequent uses of NoSQL databases:

7.3.1 Content Management Systems (CMS)

- CMS applications use NoSQL databases, especially document-based ones, to store and manage content.
- They can manage several content kinds with different architectures, including articles, photos, videos, and user-generated material.

7.3.2 User Profiles and Personalization

- Preserving user profiles and behavioural information for recommendation and customisation tools.
- NoSQL databases are adept at managing user information, such as preferences, past purchases, and activity logs.

7.3.3 E-Commerce and Catalogue Management

- Managing customer information, inventories, and product catalogues on e-commerce platforms.
- Handling a lot of product data, including attributes and variations that might not be cleanly arranged in a relational architecture.

7.3.4 Internet of Things (IoT):

- Archiving and analysing the data produced by Internet of

Things (IoT) devices, such as sensors and smart appliances.

- Massive streams of time-series data and sensor readings can be handled by NoSQL databases.

7.3.5 Real-Time Analytics:

- Analysing real-time data streams, such as data from the financial markets, social media feeds, or website clickstreams.
- Real-time analytics are appropriate for NoSQL databases because they offer low-latency data access.

7.3.6 Caching:

- Improving application speed by caching commonly used data in key-value stores like Redis.
- Relational databases and other major data storage are less frequently used as a result of caching.

7.3.7. Session Management:

- Web application user session management.
- Session data may be stored and retrieved effectively using key-value stores.

7.3.8 Time Series Data:

- Time-stamped data, such as log files, sensor data, or monitoring data, is stored and analysed.
- Column-family stores in NoSQL databases, for example, are designed for the storage of time-series data.

7.3.9 Graph Analytics:

- Examining and moving through intricate networks and

relationships.

- Since graph databases are made for modelling and querying graph-like data, they are excellent for fraud detection, social networks, and recommendation engines.

7.3.10 Ad-Hoc Data Analysis:

- Allowing for ad hoc queries and data exploration in situations where the schema is flexible.
- Unstructured and changing data can be accommodated by document-based databases.

7.3.11 Multi-Model Data Storage:

- Applications that demand many data models within a single system.
- Diverse data types are stored using NoSQL databases that support a variety of data structures (such as document, graph, and key-value).

7.3.12 High-Write Throughput:

- Applications with heavy write workloads where quick data ingest is essential.
- NoSQL databases are frequently chosen because of their capacity for handling high throughput and write distribution.

It's crucial to keep in mind that while NoSQL databases have benefits for many use cases, they might not be appropriate in every situation. The decision between NoSQL and relational databases is based on the application's particular demands, such as data consistency, query patterns, and scalability requirements. To enhance performance and data, NoSQL and relational databases can frequently be utilized in tandem.

Chapter 8: Big Data and Distributed Databases

NoSQL databases are typically utilized for analytics and large data workloads, whereas distributed SQL databases are used for transactional workloads and other applications, such system-of-record stores, where data integrity cannot be surrendered for availability and scale.

8.1 Introduction to Big Data

Big Data is the term used to describe the enormous amount of organized and unstructured data produced by several sources in the modern digital world. Volume, velocity, variety, and, in some situations, complexity are characteristics of this data. As it can be used to provide insightful insights, wise judgments, and innovation, big data has emerged as a crucial asset for enterprises, organizations, and governments.

Some credit John Mashey with popularizing the term big data, which has been in usage since the 1990s. Big data often consists of data sets that are too large for frequently used software tools to acquire, curate, manage, and process in a reasonable amount of time. Unstructured data is the major focus of the big data philosophy, which also includes semi-structured and structured data. As of 2012, the "size" of big data ranged from a few dozen gigabytes to many zettabytes of data, making it a shifting target. To extract insights from diverse, complex, and enormously scaled data sets, big data necessitates a collection of approaches and technologies with novel forms of integration.

Big data refers largely to data sets that are too big or complicated for conventional data-processing application software to handle. Greater statistical power is offered by data with more entries (rows), yet data with more attributes (or columns) may have a higher false discovery rate. The best interpretation is that it is a massive body of information that cannot be understood when utilized in tiny amounts only, but being used occasionally loosely in part due to the absence of a formal definition.

Data collection, data storage, data analysis, search, sharing, transfer, visualization, querying, updating, information privacy, and data source are just a few of the big data analysis challenges. Volume, diversity, and velocity are the three main ideas that were initially connected to big data. Big data analysis makes sampling difficult, previously simply allowed for observations and sample. Veracity, the fourth concept, denotes the accuracy or value of the data. Without enough investment in big data knowledge, the volume and variety of data may result in costs and dangers that surpass a company's ability to utilize and benefit from big data.

Here is a list of the main features of big data:

1. **Volume:** The scope of big data is enormous. It contains enormous volumes of data, which can be in the terabyte to exabyte range or higher. Numerous sources, such as social media, sensors, websites, transactions, and more provide this data.
2. **Velocity:** In the current digital environment, data is produced at a breakneck pace. Real-time data sources such as social media updates, sensor readings, online transactions, and others continuously generate fresh data that must be processed and analysed quickly.
3. **Variety:** Big Data includes many different forms of data. It consists of unstructured data (such as text, photos, and videos), semi-structured data (such as JSON, XML), and organized data (such as databases, spreadsheets). It can be difficult to analyse and glean useful insights from this variety of data formats.
4. **Veracity:** In big data, reliability and high data quality are essential. There may be problems with accuracy, consistency, and dependability because it comes from numerous sources. The steps in the analytical process that involve cleaning and confirming the data are crucial.
5. **Value:** Getting value out of big data is the main objective of handling it. Organizations may enhance decision-making, create better goods and services, and run more efficiently by

analysing this data and looking for patterns, trends, and insights.

6. **Variability:** The consistency and organization of data can fluctuate to some extent. While certain data sources are more orderly and dependable than others, some are more disorganized and erratic. Because of this variation, flexible data processing approaches are needed.
7. **Complexity:** Big Data's linkages and pattern-finding abilities can make it complex. To find hidden insights in the data, advanced analytics techniques like machine learning and artificial intelligence are frequently applied.

Organizations frequently use specialized technologies and tools, such as distributed computing frameworks like Hadoop and Spark, data storage options like NoSQL databases, and data analysis and visualization tools, to harness the power of Big Data. Big Data can now be processed, stored, and analysed on a large scale thanks to these technologies.

Big Data has a wide range of uses in many different sectors, including manufacturing, retail, healthcare, and finance. Predictive analytics, customer behaviour analysis, fraud detection, targeted marketing, and even areas like urban planning and science can all benefit from its application.

Thus, "Big Data" refers to the enormous and intricate data sets that the modern digital world produces. Organizations looking to gain insightful understanding and make data-driven decisions have problems and opportunities as a result of the volume, velocity, variety, and other features of this data.

8.2 Distributed Database Systems

A distributed database system (DDBS) is a type of database management that spreads data storage and management among a number of physical nodes, frequently linked by a network. A distributed database system disperses data over various nodes to enhance data availability, scalability, and performance, in contrast to a centralized database system, where all data is kept in a single location.

A distributed database is one that stores data in numerous physical places. It may be scattered throughout a network of connected computers, or it may be stored on several computers housed in the same physical place (such as a data centre). A distributed database system is made up of loosely coupled sites with independent physical components, as opposed to parallel systems, in which the processors are tightly tied and form a single database system.

A distributed database may be located on corporate intranets or extranets, decentralized independent computers on the Internet, or other organization networks. System administrators can spread out data collections across different physical locations, such as in a database. Distributed databases may enhance performance at end-user workstations by enabling transactions to be processed on numerous machines as opposed to just one. This is possible because distributed databases hold data across multiple computers.

The main ideas and traits of distributed database systems are as follows:

1. **Data Distribution**: In a DDBS, data is divided into sections and dispersed among various nodes or places. A distinct computer, server, or data centre can act as each node. Both horizontal and vertical table column and row partitioning are possible for data distribution.
2. **Autonomy:** Each node in a distributed database system may

have some autonomy, which allows it to function independently and take local data-related decisions. To ensure data consistency, nevertheless, there's frequently a need for centralized management and coordination.

3. **Transparency:** Distributed database systems strive to give users and applications transparency. This implies that customers shouldn't need to be aware of how data is distributed or how difficult data access actually is. Location transparency (users are not aware of the location of their data) and fragmentation transparency (users are not aware of data partitioning) are examples of transparency.
4. **Data Replication:** Data replication entails making numerous copies of the data and distributing them among various nodes. Replication can increase fault tolerance and data availability. Data consistency issues are however raised since updates to one copy must be coordinated with changes to other copies.
5. **Data Consistence:** A significant difficulty is ensuring data consistency among remote nodes. To preserve data consistency, distributed databases employ a variety of strategies, such as distributed locking and two-phase commit procedures, however they can have an adverse effect on speed.
6. **Scalability:** Distributed databases can manage additional data volume and traffic by scaling horizontally by adding more network nodes. For applications with constantly expanding data requirements, this scalability is crucial.
7. **Data Access:** Distributed databases enable distributed data access, allowing queries and transactions to incorporate data from several nodes. To reduce network latency and improve speed, complex query optimization and execution methodologies are needed.
8. **Data Security and Privacy:** Since data is transferred over networks and stored on numerous nodes, security is a major

problem when using distributed databases. To protect sensitive data, access control methods, authentication, and encryption are necessary.

9. **Fault Tolerance**: Distributed databases are created with fault tolerance in mind. Even if one or more nodes fail, they can still carry on operating. In the event of hardware or network failures, data redundancy through replication helps to ensure data availability.
10. **Global Distribution:** Some distributed databases have nodes spread over numerous geographical areas and are thus globally distributed. This enables businesses to give people all over the world low-latency access to data.
11. **Data Consolidation:** Distributed databases can bring together data from several sources, like subsidiaries or branch offices, into a single system. This makes reporting and centralized management easier.

Several applications, including e-commerce, financial services, social media platforms, and cloud computing, use distributed database systems. In addition to providing data availability, consistency, and performance, they offer the infrastructure required to manage huge data volumes across geographically distributed locations. Distributed database design and management can be challenging, requiring considerable consideration in terms of architecture, administration, and planning to fulfil the unique requirements of an organization.

8.3 Hadoop, Spark, and Other Big Data Technologies

Big data analytics is a crucial tool to get insights and enhance decision-making as firms generate and collect a lot of data. Hadoop, Spark, and NoSQL databases are three of the most used big data analytics technologies. We will give a general review of these technologies, their use cases, constraints, potential problems, and tech stack in this article.

Big Data technologies like Hadoop, Spark, and others are crucial tools and frameworks for processing, managing, and analysing massive amounts of data effectively. The combination of Hadoop, Spark, and NoSQL databases can result in a potent big-data analytics platform. Spark may be used for real-time processing and analysis, Hadoop can be used for data storage and batch processing, and NoSQL databases can be used to store and query huge amounts of unstructured data.

Big Data Analytics: What Is It?

Big data analytics is the practice of examining huge datasets in order to draw conclusions and information. Various sources of this data may include social media, customer, transactional, and sensor data. Businesses may enhance their goods and services, streamline processes, and generate new revenue streams with the help of big data analytics.

In the Big Data ecosystem, each of these technologies has a particular function to play.

Let's investigate them in greater detail:

1. **Hadoop:** An open-source software system called *Hadoop* is used to store and handle massive datasets. It makes use of MapReduce to process data concurrently and Hadoop Distributed File System (HDFS) to store data across numerous servers. Hadoop is helpful for many applications because it can manage organized, semi-structured, and

unstructured data.

- **Purpose:** Hadoop is an open-source platform created for the distributed processing and storage of massive datasets. Batch processing jobs are particularly well suited for it.
- **Components:**
    - **Hadoop Distributed File System (HDFS)**: A distributed file system that saves data across a cluster of machines is called Hadoop Distributed File System (HDFS). It is designed to handle huge files and has great fault tolerance.
    - **MapReduce:** Is a parallel processing engine and programming model. It enables programmers to create applications that process huge datasets concurrently over a Hadoop cluster.
- **Use Cases:** Hadoop is frequently used for large-scale data analytics on static datasets, log processing, ETL (Extract, Transform, and Load) operations, and data warehousing.
    1. **Apache, Spark:** Another free and open-source big data analytics software framework is Spark. Compared to Hadoop, it is intended to be faster and more adaptable. Spark is capable of handling batch, real-time, and stream processing. Additionally, Spark has built-in graph processing and machine learning frameworks.

- **Purpose**: Apache Spark is a free, in-memory data processing platform that enables distributed, high-speed data processing. Real-time, interactive, and iterative processing jobs are its strong suits.
- **Components:**
    - **Spark Core:** Task scheduling, memory management, and fault recovery are provided by

Spark Core, the platform upon which Spark is built.

  - **Spark SQL:** SQL queries and structured data processing are made possible with Spark SQL.
  - **Spark Streaming**: Real-time data stream processing is possible using Spark Streaming.
  - **MLlib:** A machine learning library for Spark is called MLlib.
  - **GraphX**: Is a Spark library for graph processing.

- **Use Cases**: A variety of applications, such as real-time data streaming, machine learning, graph processing, and interactive data visualization, employ Spark.

    1. **Apache Kafka:** Apache A distributed event store and stream processing platform is called Kafka. It is a Java and Scala-based open-source system created by the Apache Software Foundation. A single, high-throughput, low-latency infrastructure for handling real-time data inputs is what the project seeks to provide. The Kafka Streams libraries are available for stream processing applications, and Kafka can connect to external systems (for data import/export) via Kafka Connect. Kafka relies on a "message set" abstraction, which naturally groups messages together to lessen the overhead of the network roundtrip, and uses a binary TCP-based protocol that is designed for efficiency. This "enables Kafka to turn a burst stream of random message writes into linear writes" by "leading to larger network packets, larger sequential disk operations, and contiguous memory blocks.

- **Purpose**: Apache Building real-time data pipelines and streaming applications uses the distributed event streaming platform Kafka.

- **Components:**
    - **Producers:** Applications that publish data to Kafka topics are producers.
    - **Brokers**: Kafka servers that store and distribute data are known as brokers.
    - **Consumers:** Applications that subscribe to and process data from Kafka topics are referred to as consumers.

- **Use Cases**: Kafka is frequently used for event-driven architecture development, log aggregation, data ingestion into data lakes, and real-time analytics.
    1. **Java Flink:** The Apache Software Foundation created Java Flink, an open-source framework for batch and stream processing. A distributed streaming data-flow engine created in Java and Scala is the foundation of Apache Flink. Any arbitrary dataflow program can be run using Flink in a data-parallel and pipelined (therefore task-parallel) fashion. The pipelined runtime mechanism of Flink makes it possible to run applications for bulk/batch and stream processing. Additionally, the native execution of iterative algorithms is supported by the Flink runtime. Flink offers an event-time processing and state management framework in addition to a high-throughput, low-latency streaming engine. In the event of a machine failure, Flink programs are fault-tolerant and support exactly-once semantics. Java, Scala, Python, and SQL programs can be created and automatically compiled and optimized into dataflow programs that be run in a cluster.

- **Purpose:** With regard to stream and batch processing, Apache Flink is a free and open-source framework. It is intended for high-throughput, low-latency data processing.
- **Components:**
    - **DataStream API:** Developers can build sophisticated event processing pipelines using the DataStream API.
    - **Table API:** Offers a stream processing interface similar to SQL.
- **Use Cases:** Real-time analytics, fraud detection, complicated event processing, and IoT data processing are among the uses of Flink.

1. **NoSQL Databases:** NoSQL is an approach to database architecture that focuses on providing a method for storage and retrieval of data that is described in ways other than the tabular relations used in relational databases. The term "noSQL" originally referred to "non-SQL" or "non-relational." NoSQL databases store data in a single data structure as opposed to the traditional tabular structure of a relational database. This non-relational database design provides quick scalability to handle big and frequently unstructured data volumes because it is not dependent on a schema.

- **Purpose:** NoSQL databases are used for large-scale unstructured or semi-structured data storage and retrieval. They offer horizontal scalability and adaptable data models.
- **Examples**: Include Couchbase, HBase, MongoDB, and Cassandra.
- **Use Cases:** Content management systems, IoT platforms, and online applications all frequently use NoSQL databases.

1. **Apache Cassandra:** With no single point of failure and a distributed wide-column store, Apache Cassandra is a free and open-source NoSQL database management system built to handle massive volumes of data across many commodity servers. Clusters spanning many datacentres are supported by Cassandra, and asynchronous masterless replication enables low latency operations for all clients. Cassandra was created to put into practice a combination of Google's Bigtable data and storage engine concept and Amazon's Dynamo distributed storage and replication capabilities.

- **Purpose:** Cassandra is a distributed, highly scalable NoSQL database that was created with processing massive volumes of data over several commodity computers in mind.
- **Use Cases:** Time-series data, sensor data, and applications needing high availability and horizontal scalability are all cases where Cassandra is put to use.

1. **Cloud Computing's Function In Big Data Analytics**

Big data analytics has become more and more popular thanks to cloud computing's scalability, flexibility, and affordability. Businesses may store, process, and analyse enormous volumes of data using a variety of tools and services provided by cloud-based big data analytics solutions like Amazon Web Services (AWS), Microsoft Azure, and Google Cloud Platform without having to spend a lot of money on infrastructure and hardware

Modern data processing and analytics depend on these Big Data technologies. Based on their unique requirements, such as data volume, processing speed, and data nature, organizations select the best tools and frameworks. These technologies can be combined to create a potent Big Data stack that can handle varied data processing and analysis requirements.

8.4 Challenges in Big Data Management

Due to the sheer amount, velocity, variety, and complexity of the data involved, managing big data presents a unique set of issues. Large datasets can be challenging to store, handle, analyse, and extract valuable insights from. However, Big data is not always more than a certain amount of gigabytes, terabytes, or petabytes than "normal data." Big data is a relative word because the volume of data handled daily globally is always growing.

The three Vs (Volume, Velocity and Variety) play a crucial role in why big data is difficult.

The following are some of the main difficulties in managing big data:

8.4.1. Volume: Because volume can be large, it is the V of big data that is most frequently used. We are referring about data volumes that are so large they are virtually incomprehensible.

- **Data Storage:** Scalable and affordable storage systems are needed to accommodate enormous amounts of data. Distributed file systems and NoSQL databases may become popular as a result of traditional relational databases' potential limitations.

- **Data Backup and Recovery:** As data volumes grow, it becomes more difficult to manage backups and ensure data recovery in the event of errors or disasters.

8.4.2 Velocity: Velocity is a measurement of how quickly new data is being received.

- **Real-Time Data Processing:** Low-latency processing frameworks are needed to handle high-velocity data streams in real-time for applications like the Internet of Things, social media analytics, and financial trading.

- **Data Ingestion**: It can be difficult to effectively ingest data from numerous sources, such as sensors, logs, and social media, while ensuring data integrity.

8.4.3 Variety: Big data's diversity vector is made up of diverse data.

- **Data Integration:** Data integration techniques and tools are needed to combine structured, semi-structured, and unstructured data from various sources.
- **Data Transformation:** When converting and cleaning data for analysis, particularly when working with heterogeneous data types, complicated transformations and cleaning are frequently required.

8.4.4 Veracity:

- **Data Quality:** When working with data from several sources, each of which has its own quality problems, it can be difficult to ensure data accuracy, consistency, and dependability.
- **Data Governance**: In a Big Data context, establishing data governance policies to preserve data quality, security, and compliance can be challenging.

8.4.5 Value:

- **Data Analysis**: To extract useful information from massive datasets, sophisticated analytics tools, machine learning, and data visualization approaches are required.
- **Inexpensive Processing**: The cost of maintaining and processing data must be weighed against the potential value it has for the company. This is a never-ending dilemma.

8.4.6 Variability:

- **Data Schema Evolution**: In a Big Data context, it is possible for data schemas to change over time, necessitating seamless system adaptation.
- **Scaling Challenges**: It can be challenging to scale resources up or down in response to changing workloads.

8.4.7 Complexity:

- **Distributed Computing**: Managing environments for distributed computing, such as Hadoop or Spark clusters, brings with it complications for fault tolerance, load balancing, and resource management.
- **Security:** It can be difficult to keep Big Data safe from unwanted access, data breaches, and cyber threats, especially in a distributed setting.

8.4.8 Privacy:

- **Data Privacy**: When working with huge datasets including sensitive or personal information, it's important to take strong privacy precautions to ensure compliance with data privacy laws (such as GDPR and HIPAA).

8.4.9 Scalability:

- **Horizontal Scalability:** Systems must scale horizontally as data grows in order to meet rising processing and data volume demands.

8.4.10 Interoperability:

- **Integrating With Existing Systems:** Integrating Big Data solutions with current IT infrastructure and apps can be challenging and may need for a lot of customisation.

8.4.11 Resource Administration:

- **Optimising Resource Usage:** Managing computing, storage, and network resources effectively in order to save costs and increase performance is a constant concern.

8.4.12 Data Integrity:

- **Ethical Considerations:** It's crucial to manage big data responsibly, which includes eliminating algorithmic prejudice and making sure that data consumption is equitable.

It takes a mix of technology solutions, best practices in data management, qualified individuals, and a clear understanding of the organization's data strategy and goals to successfully solve these difficulties. The approaches and techniques for using Big Data will change as it does.

Chapter 9: Database Security

The variety of tools, rules, and precautions created to establish and maintain database confidentiality, integrity, and availability is referred to as database security. Since confidentiality is the component that is violated in the majority of data breaches, it will be the primary topic of this chapter.

The following must be protected and addressed by database security:

- DBMS stands for database management system.
- The network and/or computer systems used to access the database
- The database's information
- Applications that are related
- The hardware supporting the real database server and/or virtual database server.

A complex and difficult task, database security covers all facets of information security technology and procedures. Naturally, it also conflicts with the usability of databases. The database is more susceptible to security threats the easier it is to access and use; conversely, the less exposed it is to dangers, the harder it is to access and use.

9.1 Common Security Threats

The confidentiality, integrity, and availability of data and computer systems are all at risk due to a variety of hazards and vulnerabilities that are considered common security concerns. Governments, businesses, and individuals are always concerned about these concerns.

The following are a few of the most typical security risks:

1. **Malware:**

- **Viruses** are harmful programs that propagate themselves by infecting other files or applications.
- **Trojans** are pieces of software that look trustworthy but actually include dangerous code concealed inside.
- **Worms:** Malware that replicates itself and spreads throughout systems and networks.

1. **Phishing Attacks:**

- **Phishing:** Tricking receivers into divulging personal information, including passwords or credit card details, through deceptive emails, websites, or messages.
- **Spear phishing**: Phishing attempts that are specifically directed at one person or group of people.

1. **Ransomware:**

- Ransomware that encrypts a victim's data and requests payment to release it.

1. **Denial of Service (DoS) or Distributed Denial Of Service (DDoS) Attacks:**

- **DoS:** Putting too much traffic on a system or network to prevent users from using it.
- **DDoS:** Multiple infected devices working together to flood a target with traffic, making mitigation much harder.

1. **Internal Threats:**

- Attacks or data breaches started by internal company personnel, such as staff members, subcontractors, or business partners.

1. **Social Engineering:**

- Influencing others to reveal sensitive information or take activities that harm security.

1. **Man-in-the-Middle (MitM) Attacks:**

- Without the parties' consent, listening in on their conversations and maybe stealing or modifying the data.

1. **Zero-Day Vulnerabilities:**

- Exploiting software flaws that the seller is not yet aware of, frequently before a patch or repair is ready.

1. **Passwords Attacks:**

- **Brute force:** Trying every conceivable password combination repeatedly until the right one is discovered.
- **Dictionary Attacks**: Using popular words and expressions as passwords.
- **Credential Stuffing:** Using a service's username and password that have been stolen to access other accounts without authorization.

1. **SQL Injection:**

- Using a database to run malicious SQL queries via using flaws in web applications.

1. **(Cross-Site Scripting) XSS:**

- Injecting harmful scripts into web pages that other users are seeing, possibly jeopardizing their data or sessions.

1. **Data Breaches:**

- Sensitive or confidential material that has been accessed without authorization or exposed, frequently leading to financial loss and reputational harm.

1. **Internet of Things (IoT) Vulnerabilities:**

- Connected devices include security flaws that can be used to compromise data or obtain unwanted access to networks.

1. **Unpatched Software:**

- Failure to update security software, leaving computers open to known vulnerabilities.

1. **Data Loss and Data Theft:**

- Sensitive data loss or theft, whether deliberate or unintentional, as a result of data breaches, physical theft, or careless data handling.

1. **Cryptojacking:**

- Unauthorized cryptocurrency mining on a victim's computer or device, using system resources and possibly harming hardware.

1. **Wiretapping and Eavesdropping:**

- Communication lines are physically tapped or monitored by monitoring software to intercept communications without authorization.

1. **Physical Assaults:**

- Physical access to equipment or facilities can lead to theft, manipulation, or security breaches.

1. **Botnets:**

- Networks of compromised computers or other devices that an attacker is under charge of to carry out illegal actions like DDoS attacks or spam distribution.

1. **Attacks Using AI And Machine Learning:**

- Artificial intelligence and machine learning used for malicious purposes to automate and improve cyberattacks, such as developing malware or producing credible deep fake material.

To mitigate these risks, it's essential to implement cybersecurity measures including reliable antivirus software, firewalls, intrusion detection systems, routine software upgrades, employee training, and strong authentication procedures. In order to safeguard digital assets and keep a secure online environment, security professionals constantly monitor emerging risks and adjust as necessary.

9.2 Access Control and Encryption

Two essential elements of information security that work together to safeguard data and limit access are access control and encryption. They are crucial for preserving the integrity and confidentiality of sensitive data.

Here is a description of each:

9.2.1 Access Control:

Controlling and managing access to computer systems, networks, and data is the process of access control. Its main goal is to guarantee that only approved users or systems can access certain resources.

There are various different types of access control mechanisms:

a. **Authentication**: Verifying the identity of persons or systems trying to access resources is done through authentication. Passwords, biometrics (fingerprint, face recognition), smart cards, and multi-factor authentication (MFA), which combines multiple authentication factors for increased security, are all common authentication techniques.
b. **Authorisation:** After a user or system has been authenticated, authorisation controls what activities or information they are permitted to access. Permissions and access privileges are defined by authorization policies according to roles, groups, or specific people.
c. **Role-Based Access Control (RBAC):** Within an organization, RBAC assigns permissions based on roles or job functions. The access privileges of users are determined by the roles to which they are assigned.
d. **Attribute-Based Access Control (ABAC):** ABAC bases access choices on attributes including user traits, resource qualities, and environmental factors. It provides access control with fine-grained parameters based on moving variables.

e. **Access Control List (ACL):** ACLs are lists that are connected to resources and indicate which users or systems have authorization to access or alter them. ACLs can be set up at the application, network, or file system level.

f. **Access Control Models:** There are several access control models, such as mandatory access control (MAC) and discretionary access control (DAC), where access is controlled by security levels or labels assigned by resource owners.

9.2.2 Encryption:

To prevent unwanted access or transmission intercept, plaintext data is transformed into ciphertext through the process of encryption. Cryptographic algorithms and keys are used in encryption to guarantee the secrecy and integrity of data.

Encryption's essential features include:

a. **Symmetric Encryption:** The same key is utilized in symmetric encryption for both encryption and decryption. AES (Advanced Encryption Standard) and DES (Data Encryption Standard) are two popular symmetric encryption methods.

b. **Asymmetric Encryption:** Public and private keys are used in asymmetric encryption; the public key is used for encryption and the private key is used for decryption. Digital signatures and secure communication both frequently employ this strategy. Elliptic Curve Cryptography (ECC) and RSA are two well-known asymmetric methods.

c. **Secure Sockets Layer (SSL) and Transport Layer Security (TLS):** Commonly used for safeguarding web traffic, email, and other online communication are the protocols TLS and SSL, which create secure, encrypted connections over the internet.

d. **End-to-End Encryption:** With this type of encryption, data is shielded from service providers and middlemen by being encrypted on the sender's end and only being decrypted by the intended receiver.

e. **Data-At-Rest Encryption**: To protect data from unwanted access in the event that physical or digital storage media are compromised, data-at-rest encryption encrypts data that is permanently kept on disk or in databases.
f. **Key Management:** For encryption, sound key management is crucial. To prevent illegal access, it involves creating, storing, and cycling encryption keys safely.
g. **Data Encryption Standard (FIPS 140-2):** To protect data security, various businesses and government agencies frequently demand compliance with encryption standards like FIPS 140-2.

Encryption and access control work together to protect data. Who may access data is controlled by access control, and even if illegal access does occur, the data is kept private and shielded from prying eyes thanks to encryption. Together, these security measures offer a strong barrier against a range of security risks.

9.3 Auditing and Compliance

Information security and governance are key features that help firms make sure they follow laws, industry standards, and internal regulations. These aspects are auditing and compliance. These procedures entail checking to see if systems, procedures, and data handling techniques comply with predetermined standards.

Let's delve deeper into audits and compliance:

9.3.1 Auditing:

An organization's processes, systems, controls, and operations are systematically examined and evaluated as part of an audit to see if they are working efficiently and in accordance with set policies and regulations. Important auditing components include:

a. **Internal Auditing:** An organization may use its own staff members or outside consultants to evaluate and enhance its internal controls, risk management procedures, and general governance.
b. **External Auditing:** An organization's financial statements, compliance with rules, and adherence to industry standards are examined objectively by external auditors, who are independent individuals or organizations employed for this purpose. These audits are frequently necessary for regulatory reasons and to reassure stakeholders.
c. **Information Systems Auditing:** Information systems auditors are experts in examining and evaluating an organization's IT architecture, security measures, data handling procedures, and adherence to cybersecurity requirements.
d. **Compliance Auditing:** These are conducted to make sure that an organization complies with all applicable laws, rules, and standards. They look at things like financial reporting,

data privacy, and standards particular to certain industries.

e. **Risk Assessment:** Auditors review a company's risk management procedures in order to find vulnerabilities, gauge a risk's potential impact, and suggest mitigating actions.
f. **Reporting:** Auditors present summaries of their findings that include areas of compliance, areas for progress, and areas for weakness. The management and pertinent stakeholders are normally given access to these reports.

9.3.2 Compliance:

Adhering to certain laws, rules, standards, and internal policies that are important to an organization's operations is known as compliance.

Important compliance factors include:

a. **Regulatory Compliance**: Organizations are required to abide by laws and regulations that are pertinent to their sector and region. Examples include PCI DSS for payment card security, GDPR for data protection, HIPAA for healthcare, and Sarbanes-Oxley (SOX) for financial reporting.
b. **Industry Standards:** Organizations must abide by the best practices and standards set out by numerous industries. ISO 9001 relates to quality management, while ISO 27001 establishes standards for information security management.
c. **Data Privacy:** In order to comply with data privacy laws like the GDPR and CCPA, personal information must be protected, consent must be obtained, the rights of data subjects must be provided, and secure data processing procedures must be used.
d. **Internal Policies**: Employees are required to abide by the internal policies and procedures that their employers have established. These regulations could encompass things like financial controls, a code of behaviour, and IT security.
e. **Documentation And Record-Keeping:** In order to

demonstrate compliance with rules and standards, companies are often required to keep thorough records of their actions and procedures.

f. **Monitoring and Enforcement:** Continuous monitoring, policy enforcement, and rapid and efficient incident or breach response are all part of compliance operations.
g. **Training and Awareness:** Organizations must make sure that staff are informed of compliance rules and receive training to comprehend their duties in sustaining compliance.
h. **Third-Party Evaluations:** In some circumstances, third-party evaluations and audits may be necessary to verify compliance. External auditors or certification organizations with expertise in a particular industry may carry out these evaluations.

Achieving and maintaining compliance is crucial for meeting legal and regulatory requirements as well as for fostering confidence among stakeholders, partners, and customers. Auditing is essential for evaluating and confirming compliance, assisting firms in identifying areas for development, and making sure that security and governance procedures are efficient and in line with business goals.

9.4 Best Practices for Securing Databases

Database security refers to the procedures, instruments, and safeguards that secure and guard databases from unintentional and deliberate threats. Database security is to protect sensitive information and uphold the database's integrity, confidentiality, and availability. Database security safeguards not only the information stored in the database but also the database management system, related applications, systems, real and virtual servers, and network infrastructure.

It's critical to recognize that there are several kinds of security concerns before attempting to define database security. Human mistake, excessive employee database privileges, hacker and insider attacks, malware, exposure of backup storage media, physical damage to database servers, and susceptible databases, such as those that are unpatched or have too much data in buffers, must all be protected against by database security.

Protecting sensitive information from illegal access, data breaches, and cyberattacks requires database security. Strong security measures are put in place to maintain the availability, confidentiality, and integrity of data.

Here are some top recommendations for protecting databases:

1. **Access Control:**

- **Role-Based Access Control (RBAC):** Implement role-based access control (RBAC) to make sure users and applications have the right permissions based on their positions within the organization.
- **Least Privilege Principle**: Apply the least privilege principle by giving users and programs only what they need to do their tasks. Use roles that are not too permissive.

- **Strong Authentication:** Implement multi-factor authentication (MFA) for database access and impose strong password standards.

    1. **Encryption:**

- **Data Encryption:** Use encryption techniques to safeguard data in transit and at rest (data encryption and transport layer encryption). Database sensitive fields should be encrypted.
- **Key Management**: Strong key management procedures should be used to safeguard encryption keys from illegal access.

1. **Patch Administration:**

- Patch and upgrade the database management system (DBMS) and related software often to address security flaws and implement security solutions.

    1. **System Security:**

- Utilize network segmentation and firewalls to limit and manage access to the database server. Separate databases from networks with external access.
- Detect and stop suspicious network activity by using intrusion detection and prevention systems (IDS/IPS).

    1. **Monitoring and Auditing**

- Activate the DBMS's auditing functionality to record database access and usage. Review and examine these records on a regular basis for any indications of unauthorized or questionable behaviour.
- To proactively identify and address security threats, implement database activity monitoring (DAM) and database intrusion detection systems (DIDS).

    1. **Redaction and Data Masking:**

- Use data masking and redaction strategies to keep sensitive information private from those who don't need to see it.

1. **Safe Coding Practices:**

- When creating database-driven apps, use safe coding techniques to avoid SQL injection, Cross-Site Scripting (XSS), and other vulnerabilities.

1. **Backup and Recovery:**

- Backup the database frequently, and practice restoring data. Backups should be kept in a secure location and maybe encrypted.
- Implement business continuity strategies and disaster recovery plans to assure data availability in the event of system failures or emergencies.

1. **Data Classification:**

- Sort data according to its sensitivity. Apply more stringent security measures to data that is particularly sensitive.

1. **Vendor Security:**

- Examine the setup and security aspects of third-party database solutions. Make sure they adhere to the security standards of your company.

1. **Regular Security Assessments:**

- To find and fix security flaws, do frequent security assessments, vulnerability scanning, and penetration testing.

1. **Employee Education and Awareness:**

- Inform staff members on social engineering risks, security best practices, and their responsibilities for maintaining database security.

1. **Incident Response Plan:**

- Create and keep an incident response plan to serve as a guide for action in the event of a security breach. Test and revise this plan frequently.

1. **Regulations And Compliance:**

- Make sure your database security procedures comply with industry-specific laws (like GDPR and HIPAA) and compliance requirements (like PCI DSS).

1. **Retention And Deletion Of Data:**

- Create guidelines for the safe destruction of data that is no longer needed and the keeping of data. Delete or properly sterilize any storage devices holding sensitive data.

1. **Change Management:**

- To monitor and approve changes to the database configurations, access permissions, and schema, implement a change management procedure.

1. **Documentation for Security:**

- Keep thorough records of your database security rules, practices, and configurations.

Keep in mind that threats are constantly changing, and database security is a continuous process. Review and update your security measures on a regular basis to keep on top of new dangers and vulnerabilities. To be sure that your database security program is working effectively, consult with security professionals and think about requesting external security reviews.

Chapter 10: Data Privacy and Compliance

10.1 GDPR, CCPA, and Other Privacy Regulations

The purpose of data privacy laws like the General Data Protection Regulation (GDPR), California Consumer Privacy Act (CCPA), and other comparable laws is to safeguard people's personal information and give them more control over how their data is gathered, used, and shared by organizations.

Here is a summary of the CCPA, GDPR, and other significant privacy laws:

10.1.1 General Data Protection Regulation (GDPR):

- **Scope:** Regardless of the organization's location, the GDPR is an EU rule that applies to all companies processing personal data of people living in the EU.
- **Key Requirements:**
  - *Data Subject Rights*: Under GDPR, people have the right to access their personal data, ask for its erasure, and object to its processing.
  - *Data Protection Impact Assessments (DPIAs):* For specific processing activities, organizations are required to evaluate and reduce data protection risks.
  - *Notification of Data Breach:* Organizations must give timely notice of data breaches to the appropriate authorities and any impacted parties.
  - *Privacy by Design and Default:* The GDPR promotes the inclusion of data protection principles in system design and operation.
  - *Accountability and Records*: Organizations are required to keep track of their processing activities and, in some circumstances, designate Data Protection Officers (DPOs).

- **Penalties:** The GDPR levies large fines for non-compliance (up to €20 million or 4% of annual global turnover, whichever is higher).

10.1.2 California Consumer Privacy Act (CCPA):

- **Scope:** The CCPA is applicable to companies who meet certain revenue or data processing requirements and collect or process personal information of California residents.
- **Key Requirements:**
    - *Requests for Data Access and Deletion:* Consumers have the right to ask for access to and deletion of their personal data.
    - Consumers have the right to opt out of having their personal information sold.
    - *Notice Requirements*: Companies are required to let customers know how their data is collected.
    - *Data minimization*: Organizations should only acquire the minimum amount of data required to fulfil their declared objectives.
- **Penalties:** The CCPA includes statutory damages, fines, and private rights of action for specific data breaches in addition to fines and penalties for non-compliance.

10.1.3 Health Insurance Portability and Accountability Act (HIPAA):

- **Scope:** The US healthcare data protection law, known as HIPAA, governs this area.
- **Key Requirements:**
    - Medical records and other personal health information of individuals are protected by the privacy rule.

    - Electronic protected health information (ePHI) must be protected by security measures, according to a security rule.
    - *Breach Notification Rule*: Requires authorities and individuals to be notified in the event of a data breach.
- **Penalties:** Depending on how serious the infringement was, HIPAA violations can result in both civil and criminal consequences.

10.1.4 Personal Information Protection and Electronic Documents Act (PIPEDA):

- **Scope:** The federal privacy law of Canada, known as PIPEDA, regulates the gathering, use, and disclosure of personal data by businesses.
- **Key Requirements:**
    - *Consent:* Before collecting or using a person's personal information, organizations must get that person's permission.
    - Individuals have the right to request corrections of their data and to request access to it.
    - *Data Breach Notification:* In the event of a data breach, organizations are required to notify the impacted parties as well as the Canadian Privacy Commissioner.
- **Penalties:** The PIPEDA contains sanctions for non-compliance, albeit provinces may have different enforcement policies.

10.1.5 Children's Online Privacy Protection Act (COPPA):

- **Scope:** In the United States, COPPA is applicable to websites and online services aimed at children under the age of 13.

- **Key Requirements:**
    - *Parental Permission:* requires parental approval that can be verified before collecting personal data.
    - *Notifications and Disclosure:* Organizations must disclose their privacy policies and practices in a clear and conspicuous manner.
- **Penalties:** Fines and civil penalties are possible outcomes of COPPA infractions.

To preserve the rights of individuals to privacy, avoid fines, and increase customer trust, enterprises must abide by certain privacy standards. Implementing privacy policies and processes, protecting data, and ensuring accountability and openness in data processing methods are frequently involved. To manage the complexity of these requirements and create a compliance strategy suited to their particular circumstances, organizations should seek legal counsel and privacy specialists' advice.

10.2 Handling Sensitive Data

It takes careful planning, strong security measures, and adherence to pertinent privacy laws to handle sensitive data. Any information that, if revealed, could cause harm to people or organizations is considered sensitive data. Personal information, financial information, health information, intellectual property, and more may be included.

Best practices for handling sensitive data are as follows:

1. **Data Classification:**

- To start, classify the data to determine what is sensitive. Establish precise rules for categorizing data according to its degree of sensitivity.

   1. **Access Control:**

- To ensure that only authorized people or systems can access sensitive data, impose stringent access controls.
- For permissions to be granted based on job positions and responsibilities, use role-based access control (RBAC).
- For important systems and data, use robust authentication techniques, such as MFA (multi-factor authentication).

   1. **Data Encryption:**

- Secure communication protocols like TLS/SSL and encryption techniques should be used to encrypt sensitive data both in transit and at rest.
- Think about using end-to-end encryption to safeguard data from the moment it is created until it reaches its destination.

   1. **Data Minimization:**

- Only gather and keep the absolute minimum amount of

sensitive data required for the intended use.

- Data that is no longer required should be periodically reviewed and deleted.

1. **Data Masking and Redaction:**

- Use data masking and redaction techniques to hide sensitive data from non-production environments and reports, such as Social Security numbers or credit card information.

1. **Secure Storage:**

- Secure settings, such as encrypted databases or file systems, should be used to store sensitive data.
- Implement audits and access restrictions for data storage systems.

1. **Monitoring and Auditing**

- Implement auditing procedures to keep tabs on who accesses sensitive information and what they do.
- Use automated alerting to continuously monitor data access for any questionable activities.

1. **Secure Transmission**

- When sending data through networks, especially the internet, encrypt the data.
- Utilize VPNs and secure protocols like HTTPS.

1. **Regular Software Updates:**

- To address vulnerabilities that could be exploited, keep all software, including operating systems, databases, and applications, up to date with security patches.

1. **Incident Response Plan:**

- Create a thorough incident response strategy that describes what to do in the event of a security issue or data breach.
- To guarantee an immediate and well-coordinated response,

test the plan frequently.

1. **Employee Development:**

- Inform staff members of the significance of handling sensitive data securely and offer data protection training.

1. **Secure Disposal**

- Follow secure data disposal procedures when sensitive data is no longer required, such as shredding paper documents or securely wiping digital data.

1. **Data Privacy Regulations:**

- Recognize and abide by all applicable data privacy laws, including HIPAA, the CCPA, and the GDPR.

1. **Third-Party Risk Assessments:**

- Examine the security procedures followed by partners or third-party vendors who have access to sensitive information. Make sure your security requirements are met.

1. **Data Backups:**

- To secure data accessibility in the event of data loss or ransomware attacks, regularly back up important data and test the restoration process.

1. **Data Handling Procedures For Documents:**

- The collection, processing, storage, and secure disposal of sensitive data should all be outlined in documentation that is created and maintained.

1. **Legal and regulatory Compliance:**

- To ensure compliance with all applicable laws and rules regarding data protection and privacy, seek legal advice.

1. **Privacy Impact Assessments (PIAs):**

- Conduct PIAs to assess any privacy risks new projects or data processing activities may pose.

The responsibility of handling sensitive data calls for care, ongoing development, and a pro-active attitude to security. Data security should be prioritized at every level of the company, and organizations should create a culture of data protection.

10.3 Data Masking and Anonymization

While still enabling companies to utilize and share data for legal purposes, techniques like data masking and anonymization are used to protect sensitive information. These techniques entail altering or obscuring data in a way that hides the original data, making it hard or impossible to identify people or divulge sensitive information.

An overview of data anonymization and masking is provided below:

10.3.1 Data Masking

By substituting or scrambling sensitive data with fictional or masked values, data masking, also known as data obfuscation or pseudonymisation, preserves the data's shape and structure while rendering it worthless for malevolent purposes. Data masking's essential features include:

1. **Data Masking Types:**

- **Substitution Masking**: This technique swaps out private information with fictional information, such as changing real names for random ones.
- **Shuffling Masking:** Shuffle or rearrange data pieces within a dataset, making it difficult to distinguish between individual entries.
- **Character Masking:** This technique replaces particular letters or digits in data with different characters or symbols (for instance, credit card numbers are replaced with "X"s except for the last four digits).
- **Format-Preserving Masking**: Masking that maintains the original data's format while changing its values (such as keeping a phone number's structure while changing the digits) is known as format-preserving masking.

1. **Cases of Use**

Sensitive data is frequently protected during application development and testing by using data masking in non-production contexts including development, testing, and quality assurance.

It is also employed in situations when independent contractors or third-party vendors need data access but shouldn't have access to confidential information.

1. **Key Considerations:**

- Data masking ought to be reversible so that, if necessary, authorized users can access the original data.
- Masked data must be protected so that unauthorized persons cannot simply reverse or reconstruct it.

10.3.2 Data Anonymization:

Data anonymization is the process of removing or changing identifying information from datasets so that it is impossible to link the data to particular people or organizations.

Aspects of data anonymization that are crucial include:

1. **Data Transformation:**

- Identifying information like names, addresses, and social security numbers should be changed or removed.
- Combining information to classify people into larger categories (such as age ranges as opposed to precise ages).

1. **Cases of Use**

- In order to preserve individual privacy while enabling data analysis for research, public datasets, and data sharing, data anonymization is frequently utilized.

- While adhering to laws like HIPAA, healthcare facilities may anonymize patient data for research and analysis.

1. **Key Considerations:**

- It is important to carefully evaluate the level of anonymity to make sure that re-identification is either challenging or impossible.
- Techniques for data anonymization should be examined to make sure that they effectively retain data utility while protecting privacy.

10.4 Best Practices and Obstacles:

- *Finding the correct Balance between Data Privacy and Data Utility:* Both data masking and anonymization face the difficulty of finding the correct balance between data privacy and data utility.
- *Data quality*: Data that has been anonymized or mask should still be of high quality and usable for the intended uses.
- When employing these methods, make sure to comply with data protection and privacy laws, as requirements may differ by jurisdiction.
- Implement auditing and monitoring to keep tabs on who has access to what.

Chapter 11: Emerging Trends in Relational databases

11.1 In-Memory Databases

Rather of using conventional disk storage, in-memory databases (IMDBs) are a form of database management system (DBMS) that stores and manages data largely in the system's main memory (RAM). Since this method offers quick data access and processing, IMDBs are highly suited for use cases and applications that require real-time or almost real-time performance.

A database management system that largely relies on main memory for computer data storage is known as an in-memory database (IMDB, main memory database system (MMDB), or memory resident database). A disk storage technique is used by database management systems in contrast to this. Because memory access is quicker than disk access and because internal optimization algorithms are simpler and utilize fewer CPU instructions, in-memory databases perform more quickly than disk-optimized databases. When data is accessed from memory, seek time is eliminated, resulting in faster and more stable performance than from disk.

Main-memory databases are frequently used in applications where response time is crucial, such as those controlling telecommunications network equipment and mobile advertising networks. Since the middle of the 2000s, IMDBs have become quite popular, particularly in the data analytics sector. This is largely because of multi-core computers that can access massive amounts of memory and less expensive RAM.

The volatility of RAM is a possible technical challenge for in-memory data storage. Data saved in volatile RAM is specifically lost in the event of a power loss, whether deliberate or unintentional. Non-volatile random-access memory technology will enable in-memory databases to function at full speed and maintain data in the case of a power outage.

Aspects of in-memory databases include the following:

11.1.1. **Main Memory Data Storage:** IMDBs store data in RAM as opposed to conventional disk-based databases (such as relational databases). Since reading data from RAM is much faster than reading from a disk, this enables rapid data retrieval and processing.

11.1.2 Access to High-Speed Data: In applications that require a lot of reading and data, like real-time analytics, financial trading platforms, e-commerce, gaming, and content delivery networks (CDNs), IMDBs perform exceptionally well.

11.1.3 Flexibility in Schema: Some IMDBs allow schema flexibility, particularly NoSQL and NewSQL variations. This makes them appropriate for a variety of data kinds and changing data needs because you may work with organized, semi-structured, or unstructured data.

11.1.4 Compliance with ACID: Many IMDBs make sure that they are in accordance with the ACID (Atomicity, Consistency, Isolation, and Durability) standard, which ensures data consistency and dependability despite system failures or concurrent transactions.

11.1.5 In-Memory Analyses: Real-time analytics are frequently performed using IMDBs, which allow businesses to carry out intricate queries, aggregations, and calculations without experiencing the performance snags related to disk-based databases.

11.1.6 The Cache Layer: In order to speed up read operations and lighten the stress on conventional storage systems, some applications use IMDBs as a caching layer in front of disk-based databases.

11.1.7 Robustness and Persistence: While data is stored in memory, IMDBs frequently offer ways to periodically write data to disk for reasons of durability and recovery. In the event of a system crash or power outage, this guarantees data persistence.

11.1.8 Scalability: To handle rising data volumes and escalating workloads, IMDBs can be scaled horizontally. Data can be spread across several nodes in distributed IMDBs for better performance and fault tolerance.

11.1.9 Use Cases: Among the many use cases where IMDBs are appropriate are:

- Real-time data analytics and reporting.
- Systems for financial trading at high frequency.
- Delivery and caching of content.
- Processing data from IoT.
- Systems for online transaction processing (OLTP).
- Interactive games and applications.
- Location-based and geospatial services.

11.1.10 **Disadvantages:** - Compared to disk-based databases, IMDBs may have limited total data capacity.

- They may be more expensive because they require a lot of RAM to store the data.
- To avoid data loss, data persistence and backup mechanisms must be carefully controlled.

11.1.11 **Common IMDBs**: Redis, a flexible and speedy key-value store, is one of the more well-known in-memory databases.

- **Apache Ignite**: A platform for distributed in-memory computing.
- **Memcached:** A technology for distributed caching.
- **SAP HANA:** An application platform and in-memory database.
- **VoltDB:** A transaction-processing in-memory NewSQL database.

When data access speed and low latency are critical factors, in-memory databases are an effective solution. Their adoption should, however, be taken into account depending on the particular needs and financial limitations of your project, as they might not be the greatest fit in all use scenarios.

11.2 Blockchain and Databases

The blockchain-based database combines traditional databases with distributed databases, allowing data to be exchanged and stored while being backed by many layers of blockchains through the Database Interface (also known as Compute Interface). The information is accessible to everyone because the database itself is shared in the form of an unchangeable, encrypted ledger. Databases and blockchain technology both have their advantages and disadvantages.

An outline of the connection between databases and blockchain is provided below:

11.2.1. Blockchain: Using cryptographic hashes, a blockchain is a growing list of documents (blocks) that are securely connected to one another. Each block includes transaction data (often represented as a Merkle tree, where data nodes are represented by leaves), a timestamp, and a cryptographic hash of the preceding block. Each block links to the blocks before it, forming an effective chain (compare linked list data structure), because each block carries information about the blocks preceding it. Thus, once a transaction has been recorded, it cannot be undone without also undoing all subsequent blocks, making blockchain transactions irreversible.

- **Decentralised Ledger:** A blockchain is a distributed, decentralised ledger that keeps track of transactions amongst a network of nodes (computers). A copy of the full blockchain is stored on each node in the network, and a consensus method is used to update it constantly.
- **Immutability:** It is very difficult to change or remove data once it has been stored on a blockchain. Through cryptographic hashing and network-wide consensus, this immutability is made possible.
- **Smart Contracts:** These are self-executing contracts with the

terms of the agreement explicitly put into code, can be created on blockchain systems like Ethereum. Processes can be automated using smart contracts if certain requirements are met.

- **Security:** Transactions on blockchains are validated through consensus, and data is secured using cryptographic techniques. They become extremely resistant to fraud and tampering as a result.

11.2.2. Databases: A database is a structured collection of data that is stored and accessed electronically via a database management system (also known as a data store). Large databases are housed on computer clusters or cloud storage, whilst small databases can be stored on a file system. Data modelling, effective data representation and storage, query languages, security and privacy of sensitive data, and distributed computing challenges, such as providing concurrent access and fault tolerance, are all part of the design of databases.

In order to collect and process data, a *database management system* (DBMS) communicates with applications, end users, and the database itself. The primary tools offered to manage the database are also included in the DBMS software. A database system is the collective name for the database, the database management system, and any related applications. The term "database" is frequently used in an ambiguous manner to describe any DBMS, the database system, or a database-related application.

- **Centralised or Distributed:** Traditional databases can be spread (using numerous servers) or centralized (using a single server). Despite having potential single points of failure, centralized databases are simpler to manage. Greater scalability and fault tolerance are provided by distributed databases.
- **Flexibility**: they can hold unstructured, semi-structured, and

structured data. They have a wide range of uses, from straightforward record-keeping to intricate data processing.

- **Performance:** High-speed data retrieval and querying are made possible by databases' optimization. Performance can be increased by employing strategies like caching and indexing.
- **SQL and NoSQL:** Based on their data models, databases can be classified as SQL (Structured Query Language) or NoSQL (Not Only SQL). In contrast to NoSQL databases, which for some use cases offer greater flexibility and scalability, SQL databases make use of a structured schema.

11.2.3. Databases and Blockchain: Their Relationship

- **Data Storage**: Databases are used by blockchains to store transaction data. The data contained in each blockchain block, which each comprises a set of transactions, is frequently kept in a database, which could be a key-value store or another type of storage system.

- **Interoperability**: Interoperability is important since many blockchain applications need to communicate with conventional databases. A supply chain blockchain, for instance, might require data access from an inventory management database.
- **Smart Contracts**: To retrieve data or carry out actions based on real-world facts, smart contracts frequently communicate with external databases or oracles.
- **Hybrid Solutions**: Some initiatives mix blockchain and conventional databases to take advantage of each technology's advantages. For instance, whereas a typical database may perform complicated queries, a blockchain may retain transaction history.
- **Blockchain-Based Databases:** Databases built on

blockchains have started to take shape. These databases would combine the security and immutability of a blockchain with the querying power of a conventional database.

In conclusion, blockchains and databases each have unique functions and traits. While databases are designed for data administration and retrieval, blockchains are renowned for their immutability and security. They don't, however, have to be used separately, and a lot of real-world applications combine the two to accomplish certain objectives.

11.3 Containerization and Orchestration

Two essential technologies for modern software development and deployment are containerization and orchestration. They make it possible to handle apps and their dependencies effectively in a flexible and scalable way.

An overview of containerization and orchestration is provided below:

11.3.1 Containerization:

11.3.1.1 What is Containerisation?

A program and all of its dependencies, like as libraries and configuration files, are packaged into a container image through the lightweight virtualization technique known as *containerization*. Everything required to operate the program is included in this container image, making it portable and consistent across many contexts.

1. **Key Concepts:**

- **Container Images:** These are read-only templates that describe the environment and the application, respectively. Docker images are a popular container image format.
- **Containers:** Instances of container images that can be executed on a host system are known as containers. They are effective and portable since they are separate from one another and utilize the host's OS kernel.

1. **Benefits:**

- **Consistency:** Containers help to prevent "it works on my machine" problems by ensuring that programs operate consistently across development, testing, and production

environments.
- **Isolation:** Because containers offer process and file system isolation, many programs can operate without conflict on the same host.
- **Portability:** Applications can be more easily moved between environments or cloud providers thanks to containers' ability to run on any system that supports the containerization platform.

1. **Frequently Used Containerization Platforms:**

- **Docker:** The most popular containerization platform, Docker, provides tools for building, sharing, and operating containers.
- **Containerd, rkt (Rocket):** Alternative container runtimes that are compatible with Docker images include Containerd and rkt (Rocket).
- **Podman:** A daemon- and root-free container management alternative to Docker.

11.3.2 Orchestration:

11.3.2.1 What is Orchestration?

The automatic deployment, scaling, and management of containerized applications across a cluster of computers or nodes is known as *orchestration.* It makes certain that containers are set up, managed, and scaled in accordance with predetermined policies and configurations.

1. **Key Concepts:**

- **Frameworks for Orchestration:** These are the programs and devices that automate the deployment and administration of containers. The most popular orchestration framework is

Kubernetes.

- **Cluster:** A cluster is a collection of computers (also known as nodes) that collaborate to run and control containers.
- **Control Plane:** The control plane is in charge of supervising and directing the deployment of containers throughout the cluster.

1. **Benefits:**

- **Scalability:** Using orchestration, containerized systems may be automatically scaled to meet demand.
- **High Availability:** This feature makes sure that even if certain nodes or containers fail, applications will still be accessible.
- **Load Balancing:** For greater resource efficiency and fault tolerance, orchestration frameworks can distribute traffic to containers.
- **Rolling Updates:** Applications that have been containerized can be updated and upgraded with little to no downtime.

1. **Frequently Used Orchestration Frameworks**

- **Kubernetes:** The leading orchestration platform is Kubernetes, which provides a wealth of functionality for container management, scaling, and orchestration.
- **Docker Swarm:** Docker Swarm is a more straightforward orchestration tool that has a close relationship with Docker.
- **Apache Mesos and Marathon**: Alternative orchestration technologies for handling containerized applications include Apache Mesos and Marathon.

1. **Containerization And Orchestration**

Applications that need to be extremely scalable, resilient, and portable are frequently created and managed using a combination of containerization and orchestration. Particularly Kubernetes, which is used in many deployments of containerized applications, has emerged as the de facto standard for coordinating containers. Combining these two technologies enables businesses to create and deploy applications more quickly, scale them as needed, and guarantee their high availability and consistency across diverse settings.

11.4 Serverless Databases

A sort of cloud-based database product known as "*Serverless Databases*," sometimes known as "*Serverless Database Services*," makes database management easier by abstracting away the difficulties of server deployment, scaling, and maintenance. With the help of these services, developers can concentrate entirely on creating and maintaining their apps, with the underlying infrastructure being handled by the cloud provider.

An overview of Serverless databases is given below:

11.4.1 Key Characteristics of Serverless Databases

- **No Server Management**: Users are relieved of the duty of procuring, configuring, and administering database servers while using Serverless databases. All server-related duties are performed by the cloud provider.
- **Automatic Scaling:** As workload and demand fluctuate, Serverless databases adapt automatically. Dynamic resource allocation makes that the database can effectively handle shifting traffic volumes.
- **Pay-Per-Use Pricing:** Serverless database services frequently follow a pay-as-you-go business model, in which customers are charged for the actual resources they use (such as storage space or I/O operations) as opposed to pre-allocated capacity.
- **Zero Downtime:** These services are intended to reduce or completely eliminate downtime during scaling or maintenance procedures. The service is designed with fault tolerance and high availability.
- **Security and Compliance:** Serverless databases frequently come with security features including encryption at rest and in transit, role-based access control, and adherence to industry standards and laws.

11.4.2. Serverless Database Types Include:

- **Serverless SQL Databases:**
    - Examples include Google Cloud SQL (using the Serverless option), Azure SQL Database, and AWS Aurora Serverless.
    - These databases offer relational database functionality along with the previously mentioned Serverless advantages.
- **NoSQL Serverless Databases:**
    - NoSQL databases with Serverless provisioning are available through services like Google Cloud Firestore, Azure Cosmos DB, and AWS DynamoDB On-Demand.
    - These databases are ideal for applications that require adaptable, schema-free data structures.
- **Serverless data Warehouses:**
    - Analytics and business intelligence can benefit from Serverless query processing provided by cloud-based data warehouses like AWS Athena and Google BigQuery.
- **Serverless File And Storage Systems:**
    - Some cloud service providers provide highly scalable Serverless storage and file systems that are billed based on consumption, such as AWS S3 and Azure Blob Storage.
- **Use case for Serverless Databases:**
    - *Variable Workloads*: Serverless databases are advantageous for applications with varying workloads since resources are automatically scaled up or down in response to demand.
    - *Development and testing:* Since developers don't have

to worry about setting up infrastructure to create and test applications, development time is reduced.

- *Prototype and MVPs:* Serverless databases are perfect for creating prototypes and Minimum Viable Products (MVPs) rapidly and affordably.
- *Serverless and event-driven systems*: These databases are a perfect fit for Serverless and event-driven systems, in which resources are distributed dynamically in response to events.
- *Web and Mobile Apps:* Where scalability and cost effectiveness are crucial, Serverless databases are frequently employed in web and mobile applications.
- *Ad Hoc Analytics:* Without the need to set up specialized resources, users can conduct ad hoc SQL queries on huge datasets using data warehouses like AWS Athena and Google BigQuery.

Although Serverless databases have numerous benefits, they might not be appropriate in every situation. Models with reserved capacity could be more economical for applications with steady, high, and predictable workloads. When deciding between Serverless and conventional database systems, it's crucial to consider the project's unique needs and financial limitations.

Chapter 12: Case Studies and Real-World Applications

12.1 Real-Life Examples of Relational Databases

In many different fields and applications, relational databases are used extensively to store and manage structured data. Here are some instances of real-world uses for relational databases:

1. **E-Commerce Platforms:** Relational databases are used by online shops like Amazon, eBay, and Shopify to manage product catalogues, customer data, orders, and inventory. This makes it possible to track sales, stock levels, and client preferences effectively.
2. **Banking and Finance:** To manage customer accounts, transaction histories, loans, and compliance records, financial organizations use relational databases. These databases aid in ensuring data security and accuracy for private financial data.
3. **Human Resources Management:** To store personnel records, payroll data, benefit information, and performance reviews, HR departments use relational databases. Payroll processing and employee management are made easier as a result.
4. **Customer relationship management (CRM):** Relational databases are used to store customer information, interactions, and sales leads in CRM systems like Salesforce and Microsoft Dynamics. Businesses can enhance their sales and customer engagement strategies by using this information.
5. **Healthcare and Electronic Health Records (EHR):** Relational databases are used by healthcare companies to store electronic health records. While observing stringent security and compliance standards like HIPAA, these databases collect information on patients' demographics, medical histories, lab results, and treatment plans.

6. **Content Management Systems (CMS):** Popular CMS platforms like WordPress and Drupal store website content, user profiles, and information in relational databases. This makes it simple to create, edit, and publish material.
7. **Online Booking Systems:** To manage reservations, flight schedules, hotel availability, and price, airlines, hotels, and travel companies employ relational databases. These systems allow customers to make reservations and receive confirmation.
8. **Inventory and Supply Chain Management**: Manufacturing and logistics firms employ relational databases to keep tabs on stock levels, supplier information, production schedules, and shipment details. This improves supply chain management.
9. **Educational Institutions:** To manage student records, course schedules, grades, and academic performance data, schools, colleges, and universities use relational databases. This facilitates instructional planning and streamlines administrative tasks.
10. **Social Media Platforms:** To store user profiles, connections, postings, comments, and multimedia content, social networking sites like Facebook and LinkedIn use relational databases. These databases make it easier to access content and communicate with users.
11. **Library Systems:** To classify books, administer lending, and keep track of customer accounts, libraries and booksellers employ relational databases. By doing this, proper record-keeping and effective library operations are guaranteed.
12. **Reservations and Ticketing Systems:** Relational databases are used by restaurants, theatres, and other event venues to manage bookings, ticket sales, and seating assignments. Online ticket and table reservations are available to customers.
13. **Government & Public Services:** Relational databases are

used by government organizations for a number of tasks, such as tax collecting, census data management, public records administration, and permitting systems.

14. **Retail Point of Sale (POS) Systems:** Relational databases are used by retailers to handle sales transactions, control product inventory, and produce real-time sales reports.
15. **Scientific Research:** To store experimental data, analyse findings, and cooperate with colleagues, researchers in disciplines including biology, chemistry, and physics employ relational databases.

These instances highlight the adaptability of relational databases across several industries, highlighting its significance for effectively managing structured data and assisting with crucial business operations.

12.2 Success Stories and Challenges Faced

Depending on the particular industry, use case, and organization, there are a wide range of success stories and difficulties encountered while deploying big data projects and technology.

However, the following are some typical success stories and typical problems in the big data industry:

12.2.1. Success Cases

- **Netflix:** Netflix is renowned for its effective application of big data to content recommendation. In order to boost user engagement and customer retention, Netflix analyses user viewing patterns and preferences in order to provide personalized content to millions of users globally.
- **Amazon:** Big data is used by Amazon for a variety of functions, such as supply chain optimization, consumer analytics, and dynamic pricing. The business's recommendation engine is a shining illustration of how big data may increase sales by recommending to customers the right products.
- **Healthcare:** Big data has been useful in enhancing patient outcomes and bringing down expenses. For instance, the Cleveland Clinic employs big data analytics to anticipate patient readmissions and deliver prompt interventions, improving care and reducing costs.
- **Uber:** Uber uses big data to determine demand-based pricing, predict arrival times, and improve ride-sharing routes. As a result, both drivers and passengers can benefit from effective transportation services, and the company's revenue is increased.
- **NASA:** NASA processes enormous volumes of satellite data

using big data analytics, allowing researchers to analyse the Earth's atmosphere, track climate change, and even explore the cosmos. Data analysis and scientific advancements have been boosted by big data technologies.

12.2.2. Challenges Faced:

- **Data Quality:** The success of big data projects can be hampered by poor data quality, which includes errors, inconsistencies, and missing numbers. Data preparation and cleaning can take a lot of time and resources.
- **Security of Data**: Protecting and managing sensitive data presents a big problem. Strong security measures must be implemented by organizations to guard against data breaches and unauthorized access.
- **Scalability:** Increasing the capacity of big data infrastructure to handle the growing demand can be difficult and expensive as data quantities increase. It is a constant challenge to keep systems efficient and effective.
- **Talent Shortage:** Big data and data science professionals are in limited supply. For businesses, it can be difficult to find and keep qualified employees who can use big data technologies.
- **Compliance and Regulations:** Businesses need to understand the complicated web of data protection and compliance laws, including the GDPR, HIPAA, and CCPA. Utilizing big data while adhering to these rules might present considerable difficulties.
- **Integration:** Adding big data solutions to current databases and systems might be challenging. It is essential to guarantee data consistency and compatibility with legacy systems.
- **Cost Control:** Increasing the size of the big data infrastructure may result in higher operating costs. A constant concern is how to manage cost effectiveness while retaining

great performance.

- **Data Governance:** Setting up data governance policies and practices to guarantee data security, compliance, and quality may be a time-consuming and difficult task.
- **Changing Technology Landscape:** Technology landscape is constantly changing, and big data technologies are no exception. Making informed technological decisions and staying on top of the newest tools and trends can be challenging.
- **Resistance to Change:** One of the biggest obstacles to the successful adoption of big data is dealing with resistance from stakeholders or employees who are not used to making decisions based on data.

Big data projects must be carefully planned, funded, and committed to overcoming these obstacles in order to be successful. Businesses who can get over these barriers and utilize the power of big data stand to gain insightful knowledge and competitive benefits.

12.3 Lessons Learned from Large-Scale Deployments

Large-scale technology deployments, whether they involve a sophisticated software system, a data centre, or a network infrastructure, frequently yield insightful insights that can guide future initiatives and aid businesses in succeeding.

The following are some typical lessons discovered from extensive deployments:

1. **Thorough Planning is Essential:** Prior to beginning any significant large-scale deployment, extensive planning is essential. Clarified project objectives, specifications, timetables, and budgets are part of this. Early involvement of stakeholders and subject matter experts will help to ensure a thorough grasp of the project's scope and potential difficulties.
2. **Modular and Scalable Architecture:** Create modular and scalable systems and architectures. Flexibility is frequently needed for large-scale deployments to provide for expansion and shifting needs. It can be quite useful to have the flexibility to add or remove components as needed.
3. **Robust Testing and Quality Assurance:** Quality assurance and robust testing are essential components of large-scale deployments. To find and fix problems before they affect users, create thorough test plans, run load tests, and execute rigorous quality assurance.
4. **Monitoring and Analytics:** Implement thorough monitoring and analytics tools to track down bottlenecks or abnormalities and regularly evaluate system performance. System dependability can be increased and outages can be avoided through proactive monitoring.
5. **Automation is Vital:** Automating is Crucial Large-scale

deployments can be made much simpler with automation. Provisioning, configuration management, and deployment pipelines that are automated speed up operations and lower the possibility of human error.

6. **Redundancy and Failover:** In order to provide high availability and fault tolerance, consider redundancy and failover solutions. For reducing downtime, redundant components and data backups are essential.
7. **Scalability and Performance Optimization:** Recognize the limits of your systems' scalability and make growth plans in accordance with them. Optimize performance frequently to handle rising workloads and user expectations.
8. **Sharing of Knowledge and Documentation:** Maintain thorough documentation of the system architecture, configurations, processes, and troubleshooting manuals. Sharing information within the group makes it possible for everyone to comprehend how the system functions and respond to problems in a useful way.
9. **Clear Communication:** Maintain open and transparent channels of communication with team members, stakeholders, and users. Changes, updates, and problems should be communicated promptly to avoid misunderstandings and increase confidence.
10. **Resource Management:** Carefully manage all resources, including staff, hardware, and software licensing. Resources should be allocated in accordance with project requirements and financial limitations.
11. **User Assistance and Training:** Enable effective end-user usage by providing sufficient user assistance and training.
12. **Take Nothing for Granted**: Large-scale deployments can include unexpected events. Be ready to adjust to unforeseen difficulties and modifications to the project's scope. Flexibility

and agility are advantages when resolving unforeseen problems.

13. **Post-Deployment Evaluation:** After deployment, evaluate the project to determine its successes and potential areas for improvement. This is known as a post-mortem or retrospective study. Utilize these insights to improve deployment procedures and lessons learnt in the future.
14. **Security and Compliance:** Make sure that the deployment is designed with security precautions and compliance standards in mind from the beginning. Update security procedures frequently to stay ahead of developing dangers.
15. **Continual Optimisation:** Large-scale deployments are ongoing projects that require ongoing optimization. To maintain the system's effectiveness and efficiency, continuously evaluate performance, security, and user feedback and make iterative enhancements.

Large-scale deployments might be complicated and difficult, but they also present chances for development and innovation. Organizations may boost the likelihood of successful large-scale deployments and meet their strategic goals by putting these lessons learned into practice and promoting a culture of continuous improvement.

Conclusion

The Ever-Evolving World of Relational Databases

Since relational databases were introduced in the 1970s, the industry has changed significantly. Relational databases have been a key data management technology, and they are still essential to the creation of contemporary software. The following are some salient features of the dynamic environment of relational databases:

1. **Advancement In Technology:**

- *Hardware Advancements:* Relational databases have benefited from hardware technology advances that have made it possible for quicker storage, more memory, and more computing power. Significant performance improvements have resulted from this.

1. **Distribution and Scaling:**

- *Horizontal Scalability*: Traditional relational databases were usually scaled vertically by upgrading the hardware of the server. Through methods like sharding and distributed database systems, horizontal scalability has become more popular in recent years. This makes databases capable of handling heavy workloads.

1. **Cloud Adoption:**

- **Database as a Service (DBaaS):** By offering managed relational database services, cloud providers make it simpler for businesses to deploy and scale databases without having to worry about handling infrastructure management. Popular options include Azure Database, Google Cloud SQL, and Amazon RDS.

1. **Using NoSQL Databases:**

- The "NoSQL vs. SQL" argument was sparked by the emergence of NoSQL databases, which provided new methods for processing data. Many NoSQL databases, including document stores like MongoDB, key-value stores like Redis, and column-family stores like Cassandra, are made for particular use cases. Because organizations frequently select databases based on their unique requirements, the database landscape has become more diverse.

1. **Polyglot Persistence:**

- Many contemporary apps combine data from various databases for different aspects of their operations. The polyglot persistence method enables programmers to select the optimal database for each data type or use case within an application.

1. **Advanced Query Languages:**

- The relational database standard language, SQL, has evolved with additional capabilities and extensions. Additionally, some databases have specific query languages for XML or JSON, two examples of complicated data types.

1. **Data Analytics and Data Warehouses**:

- Massive volumes of data may now be handled via data warehousing solutions for analytics and business intelligence.

In this field, popular tools include Google BigQuery, Amazon Redshift, and Snowflake.

1. **Security And Compliance:**

- Relational databases now have extensive security measures, encryption, and auditing capabilities to protect sensitive data in response to growing concerns about data security and compliance.

1. **In-Memory Databases:**

- In-memory databases have become popular because they provide lightning-fast data access by storing all of the data in RAM. This is especially useful for high-performance applications and real-time analytics.

1. **Distributed Ledgers and Blockchain:**

- Distributed ledgers, which are a particular type of distributed database, were first presented by blockchain technology. These have uses in a number of fields, including supply chains and banking.

1. **Graph Databases**:

- Graph databases like Neo4j have become crucial for data with complicated relationships. Their management and querying of data in a graph structure is exceptional.

1. **Commercial and Open Source Databases:**

- Both open-source and for-profit relational database systems are still in high demand, providing a variety of solutions for businesses with various needs and spending limits.

To sum up, relational databases have not only endured but also grown in response to the shifting demands of contemporary applications. In order to serve the various demands of today's data-centric applications, they cohabit with a number of different database technologies, forming a rich and diversified ecosystem.

Table of Diagrams

1. Critical Challenges in RD with Corresponding Mitigation Strategies

Challenge	Mitigation Strategy
Data Security and Privacy	Implement strong authentication and authorization controls, encrypt sensitive data, and regularly audit and monitor database access to protect against unauthorized access and data breaches. Comply with relevant data protection regulations like GDPR or HIPAA.
Data Integrity	Use primary keys and foreign keys to enforce referential integrity. Apply constraints, triggers, and stored procedures to maintain data consistency. Regularly validate and clean data to prevent errors and inconsistencies.
Performance Tuning	Profile and analyse query performance, optimize SQL queries, create appropriate indexes, and use caching mechanisms. Regularly monitor and tune the database server's configuration parameters to ensure efficient resource utilization.
Scalability	Employ horizontal or vertical scaling techniques, such as sharding, partitioning, or clustering. Utilize database replication and load balancing to distribute workloads across multiple servers. Consider cloud-based database solutions for elasticity.
High Availability and Failover	Implement database clustering, replication, or mirroring for automatic failover. Utilize redundancy and backup strategies. Implement monitoring and alerting systems to detect and respond to failures promptly.
Backup and Recovery	Set up regular automated backups, including full, incremental, and differential backups. Test backup and recovery procedures regularly to ensure data can be restored in case of data loss or corruption
Concurrency Control	Use proper locking mechanisms and isolation levels to manage concurrent access to data. Implement optimistic or pessimistic locking strategies as needed. Monitor and resolve deadlocks

	and contention issues
Data Migration and ETL	Plan and execute data migrations carefully, including schema changes. Use ETL (Extract, Transform, Load) processes with error handling and logging to ensure data consistency during migration
Database Design and Schema Evolution	Follow best practices in database design, including normalization and denormalization as needed. Implement version control for database schemas. Use migration scripts for schema updates to ensure data consistency.
Resource Utilisation	Monitor and optimize resource usage, including CPU, memory, and storage. Set resource limits and quotas to prevent runaway queries or processes from impacting overall system performance.
Backup and Archiving Policies	Define and enforce data retention policies. Archive historical data to separate storage to maintain database performance. Ensure compliance with legal and regulatory requirements for data retention.
Disaster Recovery Planning	Develop and document a comprehensive disaster recovery plan that includes data backup, replication, and failover strategies. Regularly test the plan to ensure a swift and effective response to unforeseen events.
Query Optimisation	Use query optimization tools, database indexes, and caching mechanisms to improve query performance. Analyse query execution plans and use tools like EXPLAIN to identify and resolve performance bottlenecks
Data Consistency in Distributed Systems	Implement distributed transaction management protocols such as 2PC (Two-Phase Commit) or use distributed databases that offer strong consistency guarantees. Understand and handle potential network partitions and conflicts.
Data Migration Across	When migrating data between different database engines, use ETL processes to transform data and maintain compatibility.

Database Engines	Validate data integrity before and after migration. Test the new environment thoroughly to ensure compatibility.
Version Control for Database Objects	Use version control systems to track changes to database objects, including schema scripts, stored procedures, and triggers. Ensure that changes are documented and can be rolled back if necessary.
Data Auditing and Monitoring	Set up auditing and monitoring tools to track database activity, including access and changes to sensitive data. Establish alerts for suspicious or unauthorized activities and regularly review audit logs for anomalies.
Database Patching and Updates	Develop a patch management strategy to apply security updates and patches in a timely manner. Test patches in a non-production environment before applying them to the production database.
Database Licensing and Costs	Understand the licensing model of your database system and plan for scalability and cost management accordingly. Consider open-source or cloud-based database solutions for cost-effective options.
Database Documentation and Knowledge	Maintain up-to-date documentation of the database schema, configurations, and procedures. Train and educate database administrators and developers on best practices and the specifics of the database environment.
Data Replication and Synchronisation	Implement real-time or near-real-time data replication mechanisms to keep multiple database instances synchronized. Monitor replication status and implement conflict resolution strategies where necessary.

Copyright: Patrick Mukosha (2023), "Mastering Relational Databases: *From Fundamentals To Advanced Concepts*"

Figure 2: 1. Critical Challenges in RD with Corresponding Mitigation Strategies

Note: These mitigation strategies can help address some of the most critical challenges in relational databases, ensuring data integrity, availability, and performance while maintaining security and compliance. However, it's important to adapt these strategies to the specific requirements and characteristics of your database environment

2. 20 Important Aspects of RD with Corresponding Future Innovation Strategies:

Challenge	Future Innovation Strategy
Data Security and Privacy	**Blockchain Integrity:** Explore integrating blockchain technology for enhanced data security and privacy, ensuring immutable and auditable records. Consider advanced encryption techniques like homomorphic encryption for computations on encrypted data.
Data Integrity	**Blockchain-Based Auditing**: Implement blockchain-based auditing for data changes, creating a tamper-proof audit trail. Investigate AI and machine learning for real-time anomaly detection and automatic data correction.
Performance Tuning	**AI-Driven Query Optimisation:** Utilize AI and machine learning algorithms to analyse and optimize queries in real-time. Explore hardware innovations like specialized database processing units (DPUs) for accelerated performance.
Scalability	**Serverless Databases:** Embrace Serverless database architectures that automatically scale based on demand. Investigate distributed databases with decentralized consensus mechanisms for improved scalability.
High Availability and Failover	**Self-Healing Databases:** Develop self-healing databases that use AI and automated algorithms to detect and recover from failures. Explore edge computing for localized failover options.
Backup and Recovery	**Continuous Data Protection:** Implement continuous data protection with real-time replication and point-in-time recovery capabilities. Explore distributed ledger technologies for decentralized data recovery solutions.
Concurrency Control	**Distributed Transaction Protocols:** Research and implement advanced distributed transaction protocols like HTAP (Hybrid Transactional/Analytical Processing) to handle high concurrency and complex workloads seamlessly.
Data Migration and ETL	**Automated Data Transformation**: Invest in AI-driven data transformation tools that can automatically map and convert

	data schemas during migration. Explore data virtualization for real-time data integration without ETL.
Data Design and Schema Evolution	**Schemaless Databases:** Consider schemaless or semi-structured databases that offer more flexibility for evolving data models. Explore graph databases for complex relationships and dynamic schema support.
Resource Utilisation	**Serverless and Containerisation**: Utilize containerization technologies and Serverless computing for efficient resource allocation and management. Explore quantum computing for high-performance database operations.
Backup data and Archiving	**AI-Driven Data Lifecycle Management:** Implement AI-driven data lifecycle management to automatically archive and tier data based on access patterns and regulatory requirements. Explore decentralized storage solutions for archiving.
Disaster Recovery Planning	**Geo-Distributed Disaster Recovery:** Set up geo-distributed disaster recovery solutions with automatic failover to remote data centres or cloud regions. Explore decentralized consensus algorithms for fault tolerance.
Query Optimisation	**Query Auto-Tuning with ML:** Develop self-tuning databases that use machine learning to adapt query plans based on evolving data and workload patterns. Explore quantum databases for ultra-fast query processing.
Data Consistency in Distributed Systems	**Blockchain-Based Distributed Databases**: Investigate blockchain-based distributed databases for strong data consistency and decentralized trust. Explore advanced consensus algorithms like Raft or HoneyBadgerBFT.
Data migration Across Database Engines	**Universal Data Migration Tools:** Create universal data migration tools that support seamless migration across various database engines, including schema mapping and data transformation capabilities.
Version Control	**Database as Code (DaaS):** Embrace the concept of "Database

for Database Objects	as Code" with version-controlled scripts and infrastructure as code (IaC) for seamless database object management and rollback capabilities.
Data Auditing and Monitoring	**AI-Driven Security Monitoring:** Utilize AI for real-time threat detection and automated response in database security monitoring. Explore decentralized audit logs using blockchain for tamper-proof records.
Database Patching and Updates	**Zero-Downtime Patching:** Implement zero-downtime patching mechanisms that allow for continuous database availability during updates. Investigate self-patching databases with AI-driven patch management.
Database Licensing and Costs	**Database as a Service (DBaaS):** Leverage DBaaS offerings from cloud providers for cost-effective database management. Explore decentralized databases that reduce licensing and infrastructure costs.
Database Documentation and Knowledge	**AI-Enhanced Database Documentation:** Use AI to automatically generate and update database documentation based on schema changes and usage patterns. Implement decentralized knowledge-sharing platforms for database expertise.
Data Replication and Synchronisation	**Real-Time Event-Driven Sync:** Implement real-time event-driven synchronization with technologies like Apache Kafka or similar solutions. Explore decentralized synchronization protocols for peer-to-peer data sharing.

Copyright: Patrick Mukosha (2023), "Mastering Relational Databases: *From Fundamentals To Advanced Concepts*"

Figure 3: 20 Important Aspects of RD with Corresponding Future Innovation Strategies

Note: These future innovation strategies are designed to address the evolving challenges in relational databases and leverage emerging technologies to create more efficient, secure, and scalable database systems. Keep in mind that as technology advances, new strategies and solutions will continue to emerge.

3. Glossary of Terms

Table of common glossary terms related to relational databases along with their corresponding meanings

Term	Meaning
Relational Database	A structured database that organizes data into tables with rows and columns, where relationships between tables are defined.
Table	A database object that stores data in rows and columns, similar to a spreadsheet. Also known as a relation.
Row	A single record in a table containing data for a specific entity or object. Also known as a tuple or record
Column	A vertical data structure within a table that represents a specific attribute or field. Also known as an attribute or field.
Primary Key	A unique identifier for each row in a table, ensuring data integrity and enabling efficient data retrieval.
Foreign Key	A field in a table that establishes a link between two tables, enforcing referential integrity and defining relationships.
Index	A data structure that improves the speed of data retrieval operations by providing fast access to specific columns or combinations of columns.
Normalisation	A database design process that minimizes data redundancy and dependency, reducing the risk of data anomalies.
De-normalisation	The process of intentionally introducing redundancy into a database design to improve query performance.
Query	A request for data from a database using SQL or another query language to retrieve, manipulate, or update information.
Structured Query Language (SQL)	A domain-specific language used for managing and querying relational databases
ACID	An acronym for Atomicity, Consistency, Isolation, and Durability, representing a set of properties that guarantee reliable database transactions.
Transaction	A sequence of one or more SQL statements executed as a single unit of work, ensuring data integrity and consistency.

Schema	A logical container that groups related database objects (tables, views, procedures) and defines their structure and relationships.
View	A virtual table created from one or more tables, allowing users to query and manipulate data without altering the underlying tables
Stored Procedure	A precompiled set of SQL statements stored in the database, which can be executed as a single unit for specific tasks or processes
Normalisation Forms	A set of rules for designing databases to eliminate redundancy and improve data integrity, including 1NF, 2NF, 3NF, and BCNF
Data Indexing	The process of creating and maintaining indexes on tables to accelerate data retrieval operations.
Data Definition Language (DDL)	A subset of SQL used for defining database structure, including creating, altering, and dropping tables and other objects.
Data Manipulation Language (DML)	A subset of SQL used for querying and modifying data within a database, including SELECT, INSERT, UPDATE, and DELETE statements.

Figure 4: Table of common glossary terms related to relational databases along with their corresponding meanings

Note: This table provides a foundational understanding of key terms in the field of relational databases. It's important to note that there are many more specialized terms and concepts in this field, but these should give you a good starting point.

Don't miss out!

Visit the website below and you can sign up to receive emails whenever Patrick Mukosha publishes a new book. There's no charge and no obligation.

https://books2read.com/r/B-A-HJNZ-WTXOC

BOOKS 2 READ

Connecting independent readers to independent writers.

Did you love *“Mastering Relational Databases: From Fundamentals to Advanced Concepts”*? Then you should read *“Computer Viruses Unveiled: Types, Trends and Mitigation Strategies”*[1] by Patrick Mukosha!

[2]

In the digital age, where information technology is integral to our daily lives, the threat of computer viruses looms ever larger. "Computer Viruses Unveiled: Types, Trends, and Mitigation Strategies" is a comprehensive guide that explores the complex world of computer viruses, shedding light on their types, evolving trends, and effective mitigation strategies.

"Computer Viruses Unveiled" meticulously categorizes various types of computer viruses, from classic boot sector viruses to modern ransomware and advanced persistent threats (APTs). One of the book's

---

1. https://books2read.com/u/bPeD87

2. https://books2read.com/u/bPeD87

standout features is its exploration of the ever-changing landscape of computer viruses. It discusses emerging trends in cyber threats, such as fileless malware and zero-day exploits, offering insights into how hackers continually adapt their tactics to infiltrate systems. It covers essential topics like antivirus software, intrusion detection systems, and network segmentation. Moreover, it emphasizes the role of user education and security awareness programs in preventing infections.

"Computer Viruses Unveiled" addresses the future of cybersecurity. It discusses the impact of emerging technologies like artificial intelligence and quantum computing on both the offensive and defensive aspects of computer virus warfare. It challenges readers to think about the ethical and moral implications of these technologies in the context of cybersecurity.

This book is ideal for a wide audience, including IT professionals, cybersecurity enthusiasts, business leaders, and anyone interested in safeguarding their digital assets. It's written in a clear and accessible manner, making it suitable for both technical and non-technical readers.

"Computer Viruses Unveiled: Types, Trends, and Mitigation Strategies" is an indispensable resource for anyone looking to navigate the intricate world of computer viruses and protect their digital world from the ever-present threat of cyberattacks.

Also by Patrick Mukosha

GoodMan

Resilient Strategies: Thriving in Harsh Business Conditions
Strategic Entrepreneurship: Navigating The Path To Success
Decisive Power: Navigating How to Make Toughest Decisions
"Reigning the Boardroom: A Trailblazing Guide to Corporate Governance Success"
Fortifying Digital Fortress: A Comprehensive Guide to Information Systems Security
"Unleashing the Power of Inclusive Innovation: Transforming the World for All"
"Exploring Computer Systems: From Fundamentals to Advanced Concepts"
"Computer Viruses Unveiled: Types, Trends and Mitigation Strategies"
"The Pinnacle of Success: Unveiling the World's 20 Most Successful Brands in 2023"
"Mastering Relational Databases: From Fundamentals to Advanced Concepts"

About the Author

Patrick Mukosha is a Management Consultant originally from Kitwe, Copperbelt Province of Zambia. He has a Doctorate in Management (Strategic Management) and Masters (Strategic Planning) from Atlantic International University, USA. He also holds a bachelor's in Information Technology from University of East Anglia, Norwich, UK, and a Diploma in Business Management from Canterbury College of Technology, Canterbury, UK. Member of the Institute for Leadership Development, York University, USA (2001–08), He was elected Vice President-Midlands of Computer Society of Zambia (2004), Executive Director for VISION-2011 – a consortium of NGOs (2009 – 2011, Founder of Strategic Management Community of Zambia (2017), Vice Chairperson Mungule Ward Development Committee (2021-2026). He has worked for more than 15 years for International IT and Telecommunication companies in senior management portfolios. After finishing his PhD in 2017, he embarked on career as a Management Consultant. He has worked on several Strategic Planning projects and conducts coaching and mentorship in Entrepreneurship, Business Management, Strategic Management and ICT. He's an aggressive serial entrepreneur and founder of PatWest Technologies.

www.ingramcontent.com/pod-product-compliance
Lightning Source LLC
LaVergne TN
LVHW090355210926
848480LV00002B/342
* 9 7 9 8 2 2 3 7 1 8 6 6 6 *